Make It Lighter

ANGELA NILSEN

Make It Lighter

Healthier versions of your favorite recipes
All the taste—none of the guilt

ANGELA NILSEN

hamlyn

An Hachette UK Company
www.hachette.co.uk

First published in Great Britain in 2014 by Hamlyn,
a division of Octopus Publishing Group Ltd
Endeavour House
189 Shaftesbury Avenue
London
WC2H 8JY
www.octopusbooks.co.uk

Distributed in U.S. by Hachette Book Group USA,
237 Park Avenue, New York NY 10017 USA
www.octopusbooksusa.com

Distributed in Canada by Canadian Manda Group,
165 Dufferin Street, Toronto, Ontario,
Canada M6K 3HG

ISBN 978-0-600-62773-9

A CIP catalogue record for this book is available from the
Library of Congress

Printed and bound in China

10 9 8 7 6 5 4 3 2 1

Unless otherwise stated, standard level kitchen spoon and
cup measurements are used in all recipes.

Ovens should be preheated to the specified temperature.
If using a convection oven, follow the manufacturer's
instructions for adjusting the time and temperature.
Broilers should also be preheated.

This book includes dishes made with nuts and nut
derivatives. It is advisable for those with known allergic
reactions to nuts and nut derivatives and those who may
be potentially vulnerable to these allergies, such as
pregnant and nursing mothers, people with weakened
immune systems, the elderly, babies, and children, to avoid
dishes made with nuts and nut oils. It is also prudent to
check the labels of prepared ingredients for the possible
inclusion of nut derivatives.

The U.S. Food and Drug Administration advises that eggs
should not be consumed raw. This book contains some
dishes made with raw or lightly cooked eggs. It is prudent
for more vulnerable people, such as pregnant and nursing
mothers, people with weakened immune systems, the
elderly, babies, and young children to avoid uncooked or
lightly cooked dishes made with eggs.

Contents

Introduction

I'd like to introduce you to this book by saying as loudly as I can, "this is not a diet book." Dieting can so easily equate with deprivation and that is not what the recipes within these pages are about. Instead, the intention is to offer simple, achievable, and practical ideas that will help you eat in a healthy, balanced way, without feeling cheated.

Healthy but nice

The idea for *Make it Lighter* came from a regular feature I had been commissioned to write for *BBC Good Food Magazine*, called "Make it Healthier." The brief was to suggest a recipe makeover each month for readers' favorite "naughty but nice" recipes—potato Dauphinoise or lemon drizzle cake, for example—to provide "healthy but nice" alternatives. You'll find no surprises in the recipe titles—they are all classics, the kinds of food you love to eat but might feel a little guilty about. My challenge was to find ways of maintaining the desired taste while creating a much lighter version—recipes with less fat, sugar, or salt, the very ingredients that make them so popular in the first place.

It has not always been easy, because my starting point for each recipe was that there should be no compromise on the rich taste or look that you would expect from the original. Furthermore, I wasn't interested in using a lot of "light" alternatives to normal ingredients, because for me they don't offer the same taste experience. Where I have occasionally used them, I've worked out lower-fat ways of increasing richness and flavor.

After creating a number of these recipes for the magazine, and with current trends for eating more healthily, it seemed timely to put the collection into a book. To expand on the idea and make the book even more useful—whether you are looking for family dinner ideas, lighter ways to entertain, or guilt-free baking—I have added plenty of new recipes, such as coffee panna cotta, fish cakes, and gingerbread.

Challenging work

Working out how to come up with a lighter version of a recipe that relies heavily on fat, salt, or sugar for its taste, texture, and appearance can be daunting, and I've often begun the process by wondering how on earth it can be done. How can cookies be crisp and buttery and yet keep fat and sugar to a minimum? However, I always manage to find a way and am invariably surprised by how good the results can be when fat, sugar, and salt are removed or reduced.

However, it's not all about taking away and reducing. There's also an element of working out what I need to replace ingredients with or add to a recipe to keep it tempting. Sometimes a trick ingredient can turn a recipe around. While struggling with the recipe for chocolate brownies, I remembered a cake I used to make while living in Canada that was made with mayonnaise instead of butter. On adapting this idea, a high-fat treat became deceptively lighter. A friend mentioned that her latest way of making hummus used a whole bulb of roasted garlic and little else, so when creating the hummus recipe for this book, I experimented with this idea and found it solved the problem of providing flavor and creaminess without having to mix in too much oil and tahini.

With other recipes, success lies more in adapting how they are made. For each one I work out new ways to cook, mix, or handle it that will maintain the desired characteristics. Altering the cooking technique, for example, can often instantly lower the fat. Instead of frying vegetables in loads of oil, just brush them with a minimum amount and roast or grill them instead. You will find similar healthy cooking tips within each recipe, providing all kinds of ideas that can be used again and again, whatever you are cooking, to help you cook more healthily.

Nutrition know-how

After researching each recipe and before testing begins, I speak with a nutritionist to find out its main dangers and toss ideas around about ingredient options: what would be best to go or be reduced and what might be included in its place to make it more healthy? My shepherd's pie was transformed to a superhealthy version when nutritionist Fiona Hunter suggested substituting some of the ground meat for lentils. "You'll never guess they are in there," she told me—and no one did. For fish chowder, salt and fat levels were greatly reduced when nutritionist Kerry Torrens suggested switching lardons or diced bacon for prosciutto. I also dip into my own fat-busting skills and use tips I have gathered from chefs and other food writers I've worked with over the years, or make use of techniques and ideas I have discovered myself along the way.

All the recipes in this book have been tested, often several times, in order to make adjustments until the ultimate lighter version has been achieved. Things can go wrong during testing, but a disaster can bring up surprising new ways to make a dish even better. Baking recipes can be especially tricky, because it is the fat and sugar that keep them light and moist. My first attempt at banana bread didn't rise and was incredibly heavy. I'd eliminated too much. But having it go wrong helped me to work out how to put it right and the second attempt rose wonderfully.

Sweet temptations

Of course, there have been times when I've thought a dish just isn't meant to be healthy, such as lemon tart. But the more recipes I lighten up—and the more ways I find to do it—the more I find I prefer my versions to the much richer alternatives. My palette has adjusted to expecting less fat, salt, and sugar. This doesn't mean I don't enjoy the occasional higher-fat or sweet treat, but such dishes are not the focus of my diet.

It is important not to put more calories into our bodies than we are able to use up in energy. So to make the most of these lighter recipes, do use them as part of an ongoing, healthy, balanced diet. That means eating a range of foods from the main food groups—fruit and vegetables (a variety of at least five portions a day is recommended); milk and dairy; meat, fish, eggs, and beans; and starchy foods, such as bread, pasta, and rice—and choosing only small quantities of ones with fat and sugar. Cutting down on salt is also advisable (for adults the recommendation is no more than 6 grams a day). If you taste before you season, especially when cooking with salty ingredients, such as stock or Parmesan cheese, chances are that you will need to add very little extra salt, if any at all.

Charted data

Nutritional therapist Kerry Torrens has been a hugely supportive advisor while writing this book. She contributed to initial discussions for each recipe as well as while making them, as I deliberated over which ingredients to use in order to make each recipe as healthy as it can be. She has also created charts that compare the classic version per serving with the lighter one. In addition, easily recognizable symbols highlight other nutritional aspects. For more information, turn to page 10.

You be the judge

Although I have given careful consideration to the healthiness of each recipe, it is important to me not to compromise the taste simply to improve its healthy attributes even more. Before I decide if I'm happy with the final version, I ask myself "but does it taste good, would I make it again?" If the answer is "no," it may mean a little more fat or sugar has to be reintroduced, or something else is tweaked, until the answer is "yes." But it's when one of my tasters says they can't tell the difference between the lighter and the classic version that I know I'm onto a winner. I hope that many of the recipes in this book will become winners for you, too.

Angela Nilsen

> The more recipes I lighten up—and the more ways I find to do it—the more I find I prefer my versions to the much richer alternatives.

Symbols and charts

To highlight nutritional aspects, there are easily recognizable symbols that determine whether a recipe is low fat, whether it contains one or more of your five a day, or by how much sugar has been reduced, for example.

To help you quickly see how I have improved each recipe, nutritional therapist Kerry Torrens has created charts that give you an at-a-glance comparison of calories, fat, sugar, or salt per serving in the classic version of the recipe and the lighter one.

LOW FAT
3 g fat or less per
100 g

Recommended Dietary Guidelines

The U.S. Recommended Dietary Allowances (RDAs) and Acceptable Micronutrient Distribution Range (AMDR) are guides to how many calories and nutrients we should have as part of a balanced, healthy diet. We all vary in size and activity levels, so these figures are only a guide, but they can help you see how much a food or even a recipe is contributing toward your daily diet. For adults these are:

Recommended Dietary Allowances (RDAs)

	Women	Men
Energy (Kcal)	2,000	2,500
Protein (g)	46	56
Carbohydrates (g)	130	130
Fat (g)	25–30	25–30
Saturated fat (g)	under 10% of calories	under 10% of calories
Fiber (g)	25	38
Sodium (mg)	under 2,300	under 2,300

FIBER
One serving
supplies one-
quarter of your
daily requirements,
or at least 6 g fiber
per 100 g

ONE-THIRD OF
THE FAT OF THE
CLASSIC RECIPE

LOW IN
SATURATED FAT

1.5 g saturates or
less per 100 g

LOW SODIUM

0.3 g salt or less per
100 g

LOW SUGAR

5 g sugar or less per
100 g

LOW CALORIE

500 kcal or less
per main course,
150 kcal or less for
an appetizer
or dessert

ONE OF YOUR
FIVE A DAY

The number of
portions of fruit
and/or vegetables
per serving

FOLIC ACID

One serving
supplies at least
30% of your daily
requirements

VITAMIN C

One serving
supplies at least
25% of your daily
requirements

OMEGA 3

One serving
supplies at least
30% of your daily
requirements

CALCIUM

One serving
supplies at least
30% of your daily
requirements

IRON

One serving
supplies at least
30% of your daily
requirements

HALF THE
SATURATED FAT
OF THE CLASSIC
RECIPE

ONE-QUARTER
OF THE SALT OF
THE CLASSIC
RECIPE

HALF THE
CALORIES OF
THE CLASSIC
RECIPE

ONE-FIFTH OF
THE SUGAR OF
THE CLASSIC
RECIPE

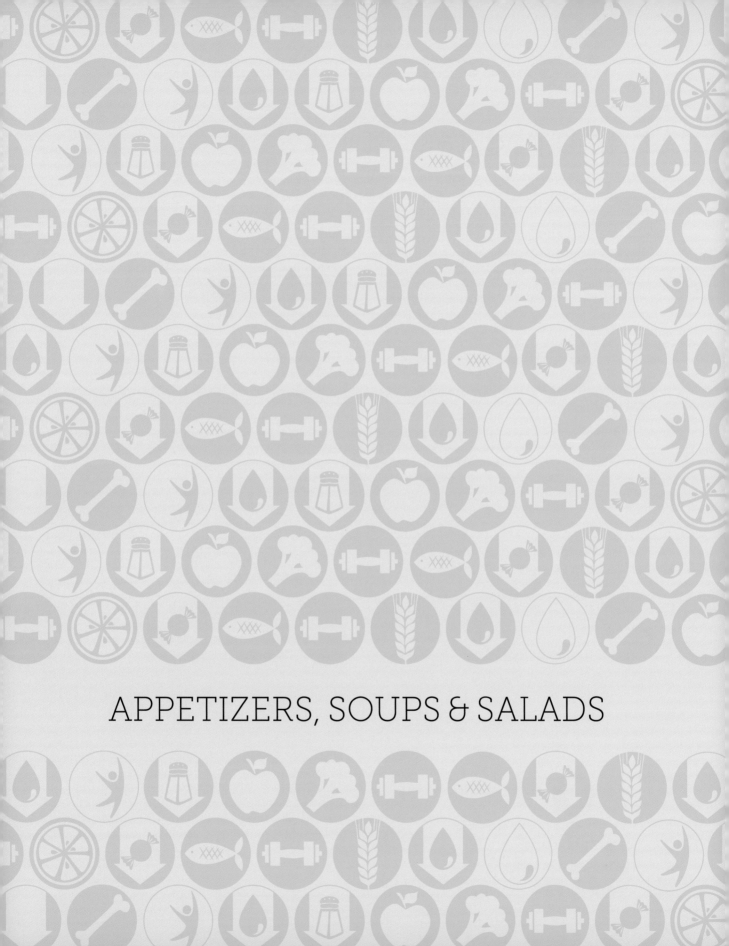

APPETIZERS, SOUPS & SALADS

Shrimp cocktail

This dish is back in fashion, so with a few updated twists, I've given it a lighter, more modern feel. Fromage blanc replaces some of the mayonnaise for the classically rich Marie Rose sauce, and mixing in flavors, such as Tabasco and brandy, means less sweet ketchup is needed. In addition, using watercress and avocado instead of iceberg lettuce boosts nutrition.

	Classic	Lighter
Kcals	303	186
Fat	24 g	13 g
Sat fat	4 g	2 g
Sodium	788 mg	492 mg

Per serving 186 kcals

protein 14 g, carbs 4 g, fat 13 g, sat fat 2 g, fiber 1 g, sugar 3 g, sodium 492 mg

Serves 4

Prep: 35 minutes

For the salad

1 lb 7 oz shrimp in their shells, cooked, to provide 7 oz peeled shrimp

2 tablespoons lime juice

3-inch piece of cucumber

1 tablespoon white wine vinegar

1 tablespoon snipped dill

1 small ripe avocado

½ bunch of watercress

pinch of cayenne pepper, for sprinkling

For the sauce

2 tablespoons mayonnaise

⅓ cup fromage blanc, Greek yogurt, or cottage cheese mixed with plain yogurt

1½ tablespoons ketchup

splash of Tabasco sauce

splash of Worcestershire sauce

1 teaspoon brandy

freshly ground black pepper

1 Peel the shrimp. Rinse the shrimp in a large strainer under cold running water, then pat dry with paper towels. Lay the shrimp in a shallow, nonmetallic dish and squeeze 1 tablespoon of the lime juice over the shrimp, then add a twist of black pepper. Set aside.

2 Chop the cucumber into small dice and add to a dish. Spoon the vinegar over the top, sprinkle with the dill and a grinding of black pepper, then set aside. Halve, pit, and peel the avocado, then chop into small dice. Spoon the rest of the lime juice over the top and toss together gently with a twist of black pepper.

3 For the sauce, mix together the mayonnaise, fromage blanc, and ketchup. Stir in the Tabasco and Worcestershire sauces and brandy with a twist of black pepper.

4 To serve, take 4 cocktail glasses and put a small spoonful of the sauce into the bottom of each. Very coarsely chop most of the watercress, leaving a few sprigs whole. Lay the chopped watercress on top of the sauce. Drain the cucumber well and spoon it over the watercress with the avocado. Pile over the shrimp, then spoon the rest of the sauce on top. Tuck in the whole sprigs of watercress and serve with a sprinkling of cayenne pepper.

Substitute some of the mayonnaise with fromage blanc

French onion soup

You might think this soup doesn't need a makeover, but the rich beef stock, butter (to create the sticky onion caramelization), croutons, and Gruyère cheese make this a heavyweight dish. This lighter version is still substantial.

	Classic	Lighter
Kcals	570	405
Fat	32 g	19 g
Sat fat	17 g	5 g
Sodium	2,308 mg	400 mg

Per serving 405 kcals

Protein 12 g, carbs 44 g, fat 19 g, sat fat 5 g, fiber 4 g, sugar 18 g, sodium 400 mg

Serves 4

Prep: 30 minutes
Cook: 1¼ hours

For the soup

3 tablespoons extra virgin canola oil

4 large Spanish onions (about 2 lb), halved lengthwise and thinly sliced

4 sprigs of thyme

2 bay leaves

1¼ cups dry white wine

1 rounded tablespoon all-purpose flour

1 tablespoon vegetable bouillon powder

For the topping

1 garlic clove, crushed

1 tablespoon extra virgin canola oil

4 diagonal slices baguette

¼ cup coarsely grated Parmesan cheese

½ cup shredded Gruyère cheese

salt and freshly ground black pepper

1   Heat a large saucepan, add the oil, and stir in the onions, 3 of the thyme sprigs, and the bay leaves, then season with a little salt. Cook over high heat for 5 minutes, stirring often. The onions shouldn't brown, just start to soften. Lower the heat, then cook slowly for 35 minutes, uncovered, stirring often.

2   Meanwhile, bring the wine to a boil in a small saucepan, then simmer for 30 seconds. Let cool. Toast the flour in a small, heavy saucepan over medium heat for a few minutes, stirring occasionally, until light brown. Set aside.

3   When the onions are soft and reduced, turn up the heat so that they caramelize, then cook for another 12–15 minutes, stirring occasionally. When they are sticky and a rich brown color, stir in the flour. With the heat still high, gradually pour in the wine and stir. Pour in 5 cups of cold water, stir in the bouillon powder, then slowly bring to a boil. Skim off any froth. Simmer for 15 minutes so that all the flavors can mingle.

4   While the soup simmers, make the croutons. Preheat the oven to 400°F. Mix the garlic and the oil together. Brush the mixture all over the slices of bread, then cut each one into cubes. Spread over a baking sheet, then bake for 8–10 minutes, until golden. Set aside.

5   Line a baking sheet with parchment paper. Mix the leaves from the remaining thyme sprig with the Parmesan. Spread over the baking sheet into a 5 x 3¼ inch rectangle. Bake for about 8 minutes, until melted and turning golden. Remove, let rest until firm, then snap into jagged pieces.

6   To serve, remove the herbs and ladle the soup into bowls. Sprinkle with a few croutons, the Gruyère and black pepper, then top with a Parmesan crisp.

use water and a little bonillon powder instead of all beef stock to reduce sodinm

Twice-baked cheese souffles

These delicious little make-ahead souffles miraculously rise again when rebaked. You can prepare them up to 24 hours in advance, making them perfect for entertaining. Switching some of the regular whole ingredients for lower fat ones or for ingredients with stronger flavor helps to transform this into a low-fat recipe.

	Classic	Lighter
Kcals	275	175
Fat	21.6 g	10.6 g
Sat fat	12.5 g	4 g
Sodium	360 mg	200 mg

Per serving 175 kcals

Protein 9.7 g, carbs 10.4 g, fat 10.6 g, sat fat 4 g, fiber 0.9 g, sugar 4.6 g, sodium 200 mg

Serves 6

Prep: 45 minutes, plus cooling and chilling
Cook: 30 minutes

For the souffles

1 heaping tablespoon cornmeal

1½ tablespoons olive oil, plus extra for greasing

1 teaspoon butter

3 tablespoons all-purpose flour

1 cup low-fat milk

½ cup grated Parmesan cheese

1 teaspoon Dijon mustard

¼ cup light cream cheese

2 heaping tablespoons snipped chives, plus extra to serve

2 extra-large egg yolks

3 extra-large egg whites

2 cups arugula, to serve

For the tomato salsa

2 cups finely chopped cherry tomatoes

½ small red onion, finely chopped

1 teaspoon tomato paste

pinch of crushed dried chiles

freshly ground black pepper

1 Lightly brush six ⅓ cup ramekins with olive oil and coat with the cornmeal, shaking out any excess. Put the ramekins into a small roasting pan. Heat the oil and butter in a medium saucepan, stir in the flour, and cook, stirring, for 1 minute. Remove from the heat and pour in the milk, a little at a time, stirring well until the mixture is smooth.

2 Return the pan to the heat and cook, stirring constantly, until the mixture thickens and comes to a boil. Remove from the heat. Reserve 1 heaping tablespoon of the Parmesan and stir the rest into the mixture, with the mustard, then the cream cheese in small spoonfuls. Add the chives, season with black pepper, and let cool slightly.

3 Meanwhile, make the salsa. Mix together the tomatoes, onion, tomato paste, and crushed chiles. Season with black pepper, cover, and chill until ready to serve.

4 Preheat the oven to 400°F. Beat the egg yolks into the cheese mixture. Whisk the egg whites to stiff peaks. Using a large metal spoon, fold a spoonful into the mixture to slacken slightly. Gently and evenly fold in the remaining whites, half at a time, keeping the mixture light and airy. Divide the mixture evenly among the ramekin dishes.

5 Pour enough cold water into the roasting pan to come halfway up the sides of the dishes. Bake for 15–18 minutes, until golden on top and risen. Carefully remove from the pan and let cool. The soufflés will sink as they cool. Cover the dishes once cold and keep for up to 24 hours in the refrigerator.

6 To reheat the soufflés, preheat the oven to 400°F. Remove the soufflés from the refrigerator about 10 minutes before baking. Turn each out of its dish and place, right side up, on a baking sheet lined with parchment paper. Sprinkle the reserved Parmesan over each soufflé, then bake for 10 minutes or until risen. Sprinkle with chives. Serve each with a pile of salsa and arugula.

Keep saturated fat down by replacing some of the butter with olive oil

•

Lower the fat by replacing whole milk with low-fat milk

•

Use strong-flavored Parmesan and a light cream cheese so you can reduce the fat even more

•

Include a tomato salsa to boost your five a day

Salmon pâté

The rich taste and texture of a fish pâté makes it an appealing appetizer—but it requires a lot of fat. By lightening the load and making a few sneaky ingredient swaps, this version becomes heart-friendly, but it also maintains all the creaminess of the classic. To keep it light when serving, offer torn pieces of toasted or grilled pita bread.

	Classic	Lighter
Kcals	225	157
Fat	19.2 g	10.1 g
Sat fat	11.8 g	3.5 g
Sodium	880 mg	280 mg

Per serving 157 kcals

Protein 15.1 g, carbs 1.9 g, fat 10.1 g, sat fat 3.5 g, fiber 0.7 g, sugar 1.6 g, sodium 280 mg

Serves 4

Prep: 15 minutes, plus cooling
Cook: 5 minutes

1 (5 oz) skinless salmon fillet

½ small, ripe avocado, pitted and peeled

¾ cup light cream cheese

2 teaspoons lemon juice

1 garlic clove, crushed

2 teaspoons snipped chives, plus extra for scattering

salt and freshly ground black pepper

1 Poach the salmon. Lay it in a saucepan, pour enough water over it to just cover, then bring to a gentle simmer, cover, and poach for about 5 minutes or until just cooked (timing depends on how thick the fish is). Remove from the heat and let stand for 2 minutes, still in the water. Lift out the salmon with a slotted spoon and let rest until cold.

2 Meanwhile, chop the avocado and place in a food processor with the cream cheese, lemon juice, and garlic. Process until smooth.

3 When the salmon is cold, flake it into pieces. Add the salmon and chives to the food processor with the avocado mix and process again, briefly if you want to keep it slightly chunky, or longer for a smooth pâté. Season with black pepper and a pinch of salt. Spoon into small ramekins or similar dishes and sprinkle extra chives on top.

Reduce calories and fat by replacing regular cream cheese and cream with a mix of avocado and light cream cheese

Shrimp laksa

With its fragrantly spiced broth, this Southeast Asian dish is a tasty appetizer for 4, or serve it for 2–3 people as a light meal. Its richness comes from high-fat coconut milk and its saltiness from Thai fish sauce, stock, and shrimp. By adjusting ingredients, fat and saturated fat are halved, the salt content is lowered, but none of the creaminess is lost.

	Classic	Lighter
Kcals	556	298
Fat	25.4 g	12.6 g
Sat fat	16.0 g	7.4 g
Sodium	2,520 mg	680 mg

Per serving 298 kcals

Protein 16.1 g, carbs 29.8 g, fat 12.6 g, sat fat 7.4 g, fiber 4 g, sugar 4.9 g, sodium 680 mg

Serves 4 appetizer bowlfuls

Prep: 20 minutes
Cook: 40 minutes

For the laksa

20 cooked jumbo shrimp, in their shells

1¾ cups reduced-fat coconut milk

2 small bok choy bulbs, sliced into 1 inch pieces

1 cup halved lengthwise snow peas

8 thin asparagus spears, trimmed and each diagonally sliced into 4

2 teaspoons canola oil

2 teaspoons Thai fish sauce

½ teaspoon packed light brown sugar

5 oz dried medium egg noodles

1 cup bean sprouts

1 tablespoon lime juice

For the laksa paste

2 plump garlic cloves, coarsely grated

1 small shallot, coarsely grated

1 lemongrass stalk, tough outer leaves removed, coarsely chopped

1 inch piece fresh ginger root, coarsely grated

1 small Thai red chile, some seeds removed, or leave in for extra heat

small pinch of turmeric

¼ teaspoon ground cumin

1 tablespoon chopped fresh cilantro leaves and their stems

2 teaspoons chili paste, such as sambal oelek

pinch of salt

To garnish

coarsely chopped fresh cilantro leaves

1 Make a stock with the shrimp shells. Peel the shrimp, leaving the tail ends on, and put the shells and heads into a saucepan with 2 cups of water. Bring to a boil, then lower the heat and simmer gently for 20 minutes. Strain through a strain to give you about 1½ cups of stock.

2 Meanwhile, make the laksa paste. Put all the ingredients in a mini blender with 2 tablespoons of the coconut milk, then process to as fine a paste as you can. Set aside.

3 Steam together the bok choy, snow peas, and asparagus for 3–4 minutes, until tender-crisp and still bright green. Set aside. Heat the oil in a wok or large sauté pan, add the laksa paste, and stir-fry for about 4 minutes. Pour in 1¼ cups of the shrimp stock and simmer for 2 minutes. Stir in the Thai fish sauce, sugar, and the rest of the coconut milk and simmer gently for 2–3 minutes, being careful not to have the heat too high in case the broth curdles. Remove from the heat.

4 Cook the noodles for 4–5 minutes or according to the package directions. While the noodles are cooking, put the steamed vegetables and the shrimp into the broth and return to low heat to warm them through for 1–2 minutes. Stir in about half of the bean sprouts and the rest of the shrimp stock if you want to thin the broth down a little. Remove from the heat and stir in the lime juice (otherwise it may curdle the broth if overheated).

5 Drain the noodles and twist in piles into 4 small, wide bowls. Ladle the broth over the noodles with the vegetables and shrimp, then top with a little pile of the remaining bean sprouts and a sprinkling of cilantro.

TIP

- If you want to use raw shrimp in their shells instead of cooked, add them to the broth in step 4 just before the vegetables, and simmer for 2–3 minutes, until just cooked.

Lower the fat, especially saturated fat, by replacing regular coconut milk with reduced-fat coconut milk

•

Make your own laksa paste and stock so that you can control and reduce the amount of sodium

•

Reduce the Thai fish sauce to lower the salt even more, while maintaining flavor from the variety of ingredients in the laksa paste

Chicken Caesar salad

Salads can fool you. You can get a surprisingly high percentage of calories from the fat in the dressing, croutons, and cheese. In this variation on a classic chicken Caesar salad, fat is kept to a minimum but the dish is still creamy and rich in flavor.

	Classic	Lighter
Kcals	674	430
Fat	47.5 g	23 g
Sat fat	9.2 g	4 g
Sodium	876 mg	548 mg

Per serving 430 kcals

Protein 43 g, carbs 15 g, fat 23 g, sat fat 4 g, fiber 3 g, sugar 4 g, sodium 548 mg

Serves 4

Prep: 25 minutes, plus marinating
Cook: 25 minutes

For the chicken

1½ tablespoons lemon juice, plus extra for squeezing

1 tablespoon olive oil

2 teaspoons thyme leaves plus a few sprigs

1 garlic clove, bashed to bruise

4 boneless, skinless chicken breasts (about 5 oz each)

For the croutons

4 slices multigrain bread

2 tablespoons olive oil

For the dressing and salad

1 garlic clove, finely chopped

1 teaspoon Dijon mustard

½ teaspoon Worcestershire sauce

1 tablespoon lemon juice, plus extra for squeezing

good pinch of crushed dried chiles

4 anchovy fillets in oil, drained and finely chopped

3 tablespoons good-quality mayonnaise

¼ cup fat-free plain yogurt

1 head of romain lettuce, leaves separated, washed, and dried

3½ cups arugula

1 oz piece of Parmesan cheese, shaved (with a vegetable peeler)

freshly ground black pepper

1 Marinate the chicken. Mix the lemon juice, oil, thyme, and garlic in a shallow, nonmetallic dish. Add the chicken and turn it over in the marinade to coat well. Season with black pepper, cover, and refrigerate for up to 2 hours.

2 Preheat the oven to 400°F. Slice, then cut the bread into big, coarse cubes for the croutons. Spread them in a single layer on a baking sheet, then brush all over with the oil. Bake for about 10 minutes, until golden and crisp.

3 Meanwhile, put the garlic into a mini blender with the mustard, Worcestershire sauce, lemon juice, crushed chiles, and anchovies. Blend until smooth, add the mayonnaise and yogurt, then blend again—it should be the consistency of heavy cream. Adjust the taste with the lemon juice and black pepper. If necessary, thin with a couple of teaspoons of cold water to get the consistency right so that it will coat the leaves.

4 Heat a ridged grill pan until hot. Lay the chicken in the pan skin side down. Cook for 15–16 minutes, turning once or twice, until cooked through. Remove, then let the meat sit for 5 minutes before slicing.

5 Keep any small inner lettuce leaves whole, tear the larger outer leaves into 2–3 pieces, then put them all into a large bowl with the arugula. Pour just under half the dressing over the leaves and carefully toss to coat. Either assemble in the bowl, or pile the leaves onto individual plates, tucking in the croutons, chicken, and Parmesan. Drizzle the rest of the dressing over and around, then finish with an extra squeeze of lemon.

A mixture of mayonnaise and fat-free yogurt make a delicious low-fat dressing

•

Bake instead of fry croutons; grill instead of fry chicken

•

Use good-quality anchovies and Parmesan for flavor, so that no salt is needed for seasoning

•

Add arugula to the romaine lettuce to boost vitamin C and the B vitamin folate

Creamy butternut squash soup

By changing to a healthier cooking technique and considering different ways to add flavor, the comfort factor for this soup remains intact—yet fat and salt are greatly lowered.

	Classic	Lighter
Kcals	436	213
Fat	29.7 g	6.2 g
Sat fat	13.1 g	0.9 g
Sodium	480 mg	40 mg

Per serving 213 kcals

Protein 6.6 g, carbs 34.1 g, fat 6.2 g, sat fat 0.9 g, fiber 8.8 g, sugar 20.1 g, sodium 40 mg

Serves 4

Prep: 30 minutes
Cook: 45 minutes

1½ teaspoons coriander seeds

1 teaspoon cumin seeds

1 large butternut squash (about 2¾ lb)

1 large onion, peeled

1 red bell pepper, cored, seeded, and cut into 1¼–1½ inch chunks

3 garlic cloves, peeled and halved

¼ teaspoon dried crushed chiles

1 tablespoon canola oil plus 2 teaspoons

3½ cups hot vegetable broth or vegetable stock

¼ cup plain yogurt

freshly ground black pepper

1 Preheat the oven to 400°F. Heat a small dry, heavy saucepan, add the coriander and cumin seeds, and toast for a couple of minutes in the pan until they start to smell fragrant (they will also start to pop in the pan), shaking the pan often so that they don't burn. Grind the seeds to a fine powder, using a mortar and pestle. Set aside.

2 Halve the squash widthwise and remove the peel with a vegetable peeler. Slice each piece of squash in half lengthwise, scoop out and discard the seeds, then slice it into 1¼–1½ inch chunks. Put the squash in a large roasting pan. Halve the onion lengthwise, then cut each half into about 8 thin wedges. Spread in the tin with the red bell pepper and garlic.

3 Mix the ground spices and crushed chiles with all of the oil, pour it over the vegetables, and toss together so that they are all well coated (hands are good for this). Spread them out into a single layer, because they will roast better than if they are overcrowded. Season with a good grating of black pepper. Roast for 40–45 minutes or until the vegetables are tender and tinged brown on the edges.

4 Remove from the oven, then pour 1¼ cups boiling water into the roasting pan, stirring to scrape up any sticky sediment from the bottom of the pan. Stir in 2 cups of the stock. Carefully transfer (in batches if necessary) to a blender or food processor and puree until smooth.

5 Pour into a saucepan and stir in the remaining stock. Reheat. To serve, drop a spoonful of the yogurt on top of each bowlful and swirl it through the soup to make it creamy.

Reduce saturated fat with simple swaps—canola oil replaces butter for cooking, yogurt replaces cream for added creaminess

Salad Niçoise

With salty ingredients, such as anchovies, and a generous amount of dressing, salt, fat, and calories can soon creep up in a salad Niçoise. But there are ways to make healthier changes and retain its sunny character.

	Classic	Lighter
Kcals	621	451
Fat	43 g	28.3 g
Sat fat	7.6 g	4.9 g
Sodium	1,008 mg	680 mg

Per serving 451 kcals

Protein 39 g, carbs 8.8 g, fat 28.3 g, sat fat 4.9 g, fiber 9 g, sugar 4.8 g, sodium 680 mg

Serves 4

Prep: 30 minutes
Cook: 15–20 minutes

For the salad

3 cups trimmed green beans

1⅓ cups shelled fava beans, fresh or frozen

4 large eggs

4 (4 oz) tuna steaks, cut 1 inch thick

1 teaspoon canola oil

16 cherry tomatoes, halved

12 pieces of chargrilled artichokes in oil, well drained

16 small, ripe black olives

4 anchovy fillets in oil, drained and finely chopped

For the dressing

1 small garlic clove

1 tablespoon lemon juice

1 tablespoon white wine vinegar

1 teaspoon Dijon mustard

2 tablespoons extra virgin olive oil

2 tablespoons canola oil

1 tablespoon flat leaf parsley

2 tablespoons snipped chives

salt and freshly ground black pepper

1 Cook the green beans in boiling water for 3–5 minutes or until tender-crisp and bright green. Drain into a strainer and cool quickly under running cold water. Cook the fava beans in boiling water for about 3 minutes, then drain and cool as before. Pop the fava beans out of their skins. Set aside.

2 Put the eggs in a medium saucepan, cover well with water, and bring to a boil, then time them for 5 minutes (for soft-boiled). Immediately drain and cool in cold water to stop them from cooking farther. Let stand for few minutes, then peel off the shells. Set aside.

3 To make the dressing, crush the garlic into a small bowl, then whisk in the lemon juice, vinegar, and mustard. Gradually whisk in the olive oil, then the canola oil. Stir in the herbs and season with black pepper and a pinch of salt.

4 Pat the tuna steaks dry with paper towels, then rub them all over with the canola oil. Season with black pepper. Heat a ridged grill pan or nonstick skillet, then lay the tuna steaks in the pan and cook for 2–3 minutes on each side (for medium-rare). Remove and set aside.

5 To assemble each salad, sprinkle one-quarter of the green beans, fava beans, tomatoes, artichokes, olives, and anchovies in each of 4 wide, shallow bowls. Lay a tuna steak on top along with 2 egg halves, then drizzle with the dressing.

choose fresh tuna steak over canned to retain more of its "good" fat and grill instead of fry it so that less oil is needed

Leek and potato soup

Loved for its richness and silky smooth texture, the reliance on heavy cream to provide that for this classic soup can make it high in fat. Using a creative choice of ingredients, this version offers a much healthier alternative that has all the creaminess and flavor but far fewer calories and less fat.

	Classic	Lighter
Kcals	428	141
Fat	32.3 g	4.9 g
Sat fat	20 g	1.1 g
Sodium	520 mg	80 mg

Per serving 141 kcals

Protein 5.4 g, carbs 18.5 g, fat 4.9 g, sat fat 1.1g, fiber 4.9g, sugar 5.1g, sodium 80 mg

Serves 4

Prep: 15 minutes
Cook: 15 minutes

1 tablespoon canola oil

1 small onion, chopped

2–3 leeks, trimmed, cleaned, and sliced

3 Yukon gold or red-skinned potatoes, cut into ¾ inch cubes

¼ head of cauliflower, cut into ¾ inch pieces

4 cups vegetable stock from a good-quality bouillon powder

¼ cup low-fat milk

4 teaspoons reduced-fat crème fraîche

snipped chives, to garnish

freshly ground black pepper

1 Heat the oil in a large saucepan. Add the onion and leeks and sauté for 4–5 minutes or until both are beginning to soften. Stir in the potato and cauliflower, season with black pepper, then pour in the stock. Bring to a simmer and cook for 8–10 minutes or until all the vegetables are tender. They should be soft, but not overcooked or they will lose their freshness.

2 Transfer the mixture to a food processor or blender and puree until smooth. Do this in batches, if necessary. Stir in the milk. Pour into a clean saucepan to briefly reheat, or if you prefer a really smooth texture, first pour and press the soup through a fine strainer.

3 Pour into bowls, spoon, and swirl in 1 teaspoon crème fraîche through each and serve sprinkled with chives and an extra grating of black pepper.

TIP

- To clean the leeks, cut each one lengthwise just deep enough so that you can open it out, then rinse them under cold running water to wash out any grit or soil.

Instead of cream, use cauliflower, milk, and reduced-fat crème fraîche to provide the creaminess and reduce the calories, fat, and saturated fat

Potato salad

It's not the potatoes that make this picnic classic unhealthy; the problem is all the mayonnaise and cream. This homemade version is easy and just as satisfying. Keep the potato skins on to boost the fiber.

	Classic	Lighter
Kcals	370	215
Fat	32.4 g	12.1 g
Sat fat	3.7 g	2.7 g
Sodium	360 mg	200 mg

Per serving 215 kcals

Protein 4.5 g, carbs 21.9 g, fat 12.1 g, sat fat 2.7 g, fiber 2 g, sugar 4.5 g, sodium 200 mg

Serves 6

Prep: 10 minutes
Cook: 10 minutes

1 lb 10 oz new potatoes, unpeeled and scrubbed

2 tablespoons good-quality mayonnaise

3 tablespoons plain yogurt

3 tablespoons reduced-fat crème fraîche or Greek yogurt

1 teaspoon Dijon mustard

1 tablespoon low-fat milk

8 scallions, ends trimmed, halved lengthwise, and sliced

3 tablespoons snipped chives

1 tablespoon chopped tarragon

salt and freshly ground black pepper

1 Cut the potatoes into 1–1¼ inch chunks so that they are all the same size and will cook evenly. Put them into a saucepan of boiling water. Once the water has returned to a boil, lower the heat slightly and cook for about 10 minutes or until just cooked and still keeping their shape. Transfer to a colander to drain well, then transfer to a large serving bowl.

2 While the potatoes are cooking, mix together the mayonnaise, yogurt, crème fraîche, mustard, and milk. Add the scallions, then most of the chives and tarragon to the potatoes. Season with black pepper and a pinch of salt.

3 Spoon the dressing over the potatoes while they are still warm, then toss gently together so that they are well coated but don't break up. Sprinkle with the remaining chives and tarragon. Cover and chill in the refrigerator. For the best flavor, remove from the refrigerator 15–20 minutes before serving.

use mayo with yogurt and reduced-fat crème fraîche for a creamy-tasting, but low-fat dressing

Coronation chicken

Originally created for a celebratory lunch for the coronation of HM Queen Elizabeth II in 1953, this British dish is a curious mix of East meets West. For a contemporary take on a classic, I've come up with this lighter version using fresh, modern ingredients. As an alternative to rice, try serving it with couscous mixed with chopped fresh cilantro leaves instead.

	Classic	Lighter
Kcals	797	402
Fat	65 g	23 g
Sat fat	14 g	5 g
Sodium	612 mg	212 mg

Per serving 402 kcals

Protein 35.2 g, carbs 15 g, fat 23 g, sat fat 5 g, fiber 3 g, sugar 14 g, sodium 212 mg

Serves 6

Prep: 30 minutes, plus cooling
Cook: 2 hours 5 minutes

For the chicken

1 whole chicken (about 3½ lb)

2 small onions, coarsely chopped

1 carrot, coarsely sliced

4 sprigs of tarragon

2 bay leaves

For the sauce

1 tablespoon canola oil

4 teaspoons medium curry powder

2 teaspoons tomato paste

6 dried apricots, quartered

1 teaspoon packed light brown sugar

1 tablespoon lime juice

100 g (4 oz) mayonnaise

1 cup low-fat fromage blanc, Greek yogurt, or cottage cheese mixed with plain yogurt

For the salad

6 scallions

1 cup chopped fresh cilantro leaves

1 ripe medium mango, pitted, peeled, and sliced

2 cups watercress, arugula, or other peppery greens

freshly ground black pepper

1 Put the chicken into a large saucepan, then pour in enough cold water to just cover. Drop half the chopped onion into the pan with the carrot, tarragon, and bay leaves. Cover and bring to a boil, then lower to a gentle simmer for about 1¾ hours or until the chicken is cooked (the legs will fall easily away from the body). Remove from the heat, but keep the chicken in the liquid to cool for about 3 hours. When cold, lift the chicken out of the stock, then strain (skim off any fat from the stock) and keep 1 cup for the sauce. This can be done a day ahead and chilled. The excess stock can be chilled, then frozen.

2 To make the sauce, heat the oil in a small saucepan, add the remaining chopped onion, and sauté for 5–8 minutes, until softened and pale golden. Stir in the curry powder and cook for 1 minute, stirring. Pour in the reserved chicken stock, then stir in the tomato paste. Cover and simmer for 10 minutes.

3 Meanwhile, put the apricots in a small saucepan with enough water to just cover them, then simmer for 15 minutes. Drain, reserving 1 tablespoon of the liquid. Puree the apricots in a small blender with the reserved liquid, then press through a strainer (you should get about 1 tablespoon of puree).

4 Remove the curry sauce from the heat, then stir in the sugar. Strain through a strainer, pressing as much through as you can with a wooden spoon, then stir in the lime juice and apricot puree and let rest until cold.

5 Mix together the mayonnaise and fromage blanc, then stir in the cold curry sauce. Season to taste with a good grinding of black pepper.

6 Cut the scallions into long, slim slivers, then set aside. If you want them to curl, put into a bowl of iced water while you finish the salad. Remove the skin from the chicken. Strip the meat off the bones in chunky pieces, remove the breasts separately, and thickly slice. Gently toss the chicken with the curried sauce, the cilantro, and most of the mango. Sprinkle the watercress onto a plate. Spoon the chicken mix on top, tuck in the rest of the mango, and finish with a pile of (drained) scallion slivers.

Lower fat by replacing some mayo with fromage frais

•

Poach the chicken and remove the skin
to reduce fat farther

•

Add flavor with cilantro, mango, and watercress

Greek salad

This fresh-tasting, crunchy salad is not short on healthy ingredients, but you do need to watch the level of sodium from the olives and feta cheese, and fat from the amount of oil used in the dressing. With a few tweaks, twists, and additions designed to keep the salad interestingly flavored, fat, sodium, and calories have all been lowered.

	Classic	Lighter
Kcals	350	254
Fat	30.9 g	18.6 g
Sat fat	9.8 g	6.3 g
Sodium	880 mg	680 mg

Per serving 254 kcals

Protein 8.7 g, carbs 12.8 g, fat 18.6 g, sat fat 6.3 g, fiber 5.6 g, sugar 11.1 g, sodium 680 mg

Serves 4

Prep: 20 minutes, plus cooling and marinating
Cook: 35 minutes

Add bell peppers to increase the vitamin c and flavor, and watercress to improve folate and up your five a day

2 red bell peppers

2 tablespoons extra virgin olive oil

1 tablespoon canola oil

1½ tablespoons lemon juice

½ teaspoon dried oregano

½ cucumber

4 ripe tomatoes

½ small red onion, peeled

3 cups watercress or other salad greens

12 kalamata olives

5 oz Greek feta cheese

2 small sprigs of fresh oregano and mint, leaves stripped and coarsely chopped

salt and freshly ground black pepper

1 Preheat the oven to 400°F. Put a piece of parchment paper onto a small baking sheet, lay the whole bell peppers on it, and roast them for about 35 minutes, turning occasionally, or until softened and the skins are blackened all over.

2 Transfer the bell peppers to a heatproof bowl, cover tightly with plastic wrap, and let cool. The steam that is created in the bowl will make the bell peppers easier to peel. When the bell peppers are cool enough to handle, remove them from the bowl and peel off the skins, keeping any juices in the bowl. Pull the bell peppers open, pour any more inside juices into the bowl, and remove and discard the cores and seeds. Cut the bell peppers into strips and lay them in a shallow, nonmetallic dish.

3 Make the dressing. Pour both the oils and the lemon juice into the bowl with the bell pepper juices. Whisk them together with the dried oregano and season with black pepper and a pinch of salt. Pour this dressing over the bell pepper strips, cover, and let marinate for at least 15 minutes or overnight, if you prefer.

4 To serve, chop the cucumber and tomatoes into chunky pieces. Halve the onion half lengthwise, then, with the cut face down on the cutting board, slice into wafer-thin slices. Coarsely chop the watercress and divide it among 4 bowls. Sprinkle the cucumber, tomato chunks, onion slices, and olives over the top. Crumble the feta into bite-size pieces and sprinkle it over each salad. Spoon the marinaded bell peppers over and finish with a grinding of black pepper and the fresh oregano and mint, then let the salad sit for a few minutes for the flavors to blend before serving.

Fish chowder

A great recipe for a simple, light dinner. The real bonus here is that the creamy broth contains significantly less saturated fat than can be found in a classic equivalent using heavy cream. Adding the fresh thyme, crushed chiles, and prosciutto gives the dish an extra kick and reduces the need for too much salt.

	Classic	Lighter
Kcals	482	398
Fat	25.2 g	15.4 g
Sat fat	11.2 g	3.3 g
Sodium	880 mg	360 mg

Per serving 398 kcals

Protein 31.9 g, carbs 32.1 g, fat 15.4 g, sat fat 3.3 g, fiber 7.1 g, sugar 4.5 g, sodium 360 mg

Serves 4

Prep: 20 minutes
Cook: 35 minutes

1½ tablespoons canola oil

3 slices prosciutto, trimmed of excess fat, cut into strips

3 leeks, trimmed, cleaned, and thinly sliced

2 plump garlic cloves, finely chopped

3 sprigs of thyme (preferably lemon thyme), plus extra leaves to garnish

2 bay leaves

6 Yukon gold or red-skinned potatoes, unpeeled, scrubbed and sliced ¼ inch thick

2½ cups hot vegetable stock from a good-quality cube or bouillon powder

good pinch of crushed dried chiles

9 oz skinless salmon fillets

9 oz skinless Alaskan pollock or cod fillets

3 tablespoons reduced-fat crème fraîche or Greek yogurt

salt and freshly ground black pepper

snipped chives, to garnish

1 Heat 1 tablespoon of the oil in a large, deep sauté pan. Add the prosciutto and cook for 2 minutes, until crisp. Remove with a slotted spoon, letting any excess oil drain back into the pan. Set aside. Add the rest of the oil to the pan and sauté the leeks, garlic, thyme, and bay leaves for 2–3 minutes, until the leeks start to soften but still retain their vivid color.

2 Add the potatoes and sauté for 2 minutes, turning occasionally. Pour in the stock plus an extra ½ cup boiling water, and gently press the potatoes down so that they are just covered. Bring to a boil. Boil vigorously, uncovered, over high heat for 10 minutes, until the potatoes are almost cooked. The liquid should have thickened slightly. Sprinkle in the crushed chiles, some black pepper, and a pinch of salt.

3 Lower the heat to medium and lay the fish fillets on top of the potatoes. Season the fish with black pepper and gently press down so that the fillets are only just submerged. Cover and simmer for about 5 minutes or until the fish is almost cooked. Remove from the heat and let sit for another 5–10 minutes. Remove the thyme and bay leaves. Still off the heat, spoon in the crème fraîche and gently swirl around until the broth looks creamy.

4 To serve, gently reheat. Divide the potatoes and fish in large pieces into shallow bowls. Spoon the broth around and sprinkle with chives, thyme leaves, and the prosciutto.

use salmon as well as white fish to give this dish a good helping of omega-3 fatty acids, which are good for heart health

HEALTHY, SATISFYING FAMILY MEALS

Risotto with squash and sage

A bowl of classic Italian risotto can be a healthy option—if you cut back on the fat, you can still achieve the rich creaminess we all associate with this comfort-food favorite.

	Classic	Lighter
Kcals	725	517
Fat	32 g	15 g
Sat fat	16 g	5 g
Sodium	1,348 mg	148 mg

Per serving 517 kcals

Protein 15 g, carbs 85 g, fat 15 g, sat fat 5 g, fiber 5 g, sugar 10 g, sodium 148 mg

Serves 4

Prep: 35 minutes
Cook: 35–40 minutes

8½ cups low-sodium vegetable stock

4 slices dried porcini

2½ tablespoons olive oil

1 onion, finely chopped

2 garlic cloves, finely chopped

6 sage leaves, finely chopped, plus extra leaves to garnish

2 sprigs of thyme

½ large butternut squash (about 1 lb 9 oz), peeled, seeded, and cut into 1 inch cubes

1¾ cups risotto rice

1¼ cups dry white wine

handful of flat leaf parsley, chopped

½ cup grated Parmesan cheese

2 tablespoons light mascarpone cheese

freshly ground black pepper

1 Pour the stock into a saucepan, add the porcini, and bring to a gentle simmer.

2 Heat 2 tablespoons of the oil in a heavy, wide saucepan. Add the onion, garlic, sage, thyme, and squash, then gently sauté for about 10 minutes, until the squash is almost tender, stirring occasionally, so that it doesn't stick or burn. With the heat on medium, add the rice to the pan. Stir for 3–4 minutes to toast it without coloring. Pour in the wine and stir everything for 1 minute.

3 Start to add the hot stock (leaving the porcini behind); this should take 18–20 minutes. Stir in 1½ ladlefuls and adjust the heat so that it simmers. Keep stirring and scraping down the sides of the pan. Once the first ladleful of stock has been absorbed, add another, continuing to stir to keep the risotto creamy. Continue adding and stirring in a ladleful of stock as each previous one is absorbed (it's ready for more when you drag the spoon across the bottom of the pan and it leaves a clear line). As the last of the stock goes in (keep a little back), check if the rice is ready—it should be soft with a slight bite—and the consistency fluid. Season with black pepper.

4 Remove the pan from the heat. Add the final splash of stock to keep the risotto moist, sprinkle with the parsley and half of the Parmesan, then spoon the mascarpone on top. With the lid on, let the risotto sit for 3–4 minutes to rest.

5 Meanwhile, heat the remaining oil in a small skillet. Add the extra sage leaves, then sauté for a few seconds until starting to brown. Transfer to paper towels with a slotted spoon to drain. Spoon the risotto into bowls, then sprinkle with the rest of the Parmesan and the crisp sage leaves.

Try a small amount of light mascarpone for richness instead of extra Parmesan

Moussaka

With its layers of meaty sauce, fried eggplant, and cheesy white sauce, there is a lot to lighten in this dish. However, you can still keep the eggplant rich without frying and using a lot of fat. With a few other changes to make the layers still complement each other but in a lighter way, the topping remains tangy, the meat light and spicy, and the eggplant creamy.

	Classic	Lighter
Kcals	820	325
Fat	58 g	15 g
Sat fat	24 g	5 g
Sodium	424 mg	260 mg

Per serving 325 kcals

Protein 28 g, carbs 19 g, fat 15 g, sat fat 5 g, fiber 6 g, sugar 14 g, sodium 260 mg

Serves 6

Prep: 30 minutes
Cook: 2 hours 5 minutes

2½ tablespoons olive oil

1 onion, chopped

2 plump garlic cloves, finely chopped

2½ cups diced carrots

1 lb lean ground beef

½ cup dry white wine

1 teaspoon ground cinnamon, plus extra for sprinkling

¼ teaspoon ground allspice

1 (14½ oz) can plum tomatoes

2 tablespoons tomato paste

1 heaping tablespoon chopped oregano leaves

2 good handfuls of chopped flat leaf parsley, plus extra to garnish

1 tablespoon lemon juice

3 small eggplants, trimmed

For the topping

2 large eggs

1⅔ cups low-fat Greek yogurt

1 tablespoon cornstarch

½ cup grated Parmesan cheese

halved cherry tomatoes, thinly sliced red onion, and arugula salad, to serve

salt and freshly ground black pepper

1 Heat 1 tablespoon of the oil in a large, wide sauté pan. Add the onion and garlic, then sauté for 6–8 minutes, until turning golden. Add the carrots and cook for another 2 minutes. Stir the meat into the pan, breaking it up as you stir. Cook and stir over high heat until the meat is no longer pink.

2 Pour in the wine and briefly cook until most of the liquid has evaporated. Stir in the cinnamon and allspice. Add the tomatoes, tomato paste, and 1 tablespoon water (mixed with any juices left in the can), then stir to break up the tomatoes. Season with some black pepper, add the oregano and half of the parsley, and cover, then simmer on low heat for 50 minutes, stirring occasionally. Season to taste. Mix in the remaining parsley. The sauce can be refrigerated overnight at this stage.

3 While the meat cooks (unless you are doing this a day ahead), prepare the eggplants. Preheat the oven to 400°F. Brush a little of the remaining oil onto 2 large baking sheets. Mix the rest of the oil with the lemon juice. Slice the eggplants into ½ inch-thick lengthwise slices, then lay them on the oiled baking sheets. Brush with the oil and lemon mix, then season with black pepper. Bake for 20–25 minutes, until soft, then set aside. Reduce the oven temperature to 350°F.

4 Spread 2 big spoonfuls of the meat mixture on the bottom of an ovenproof dish (about 11 x 8 x 2½ inches). Lay the eggplant slices on top, slightly overlapping. Spoon the rest of the meat mixture on top.

5 Beat the eggs in a bowl. Spoon a little of the yogurt into a separate bowl and stir in the cornstarch, then stir in the remaining yogurt. Mix this into the eggs with half of the cheese. Season with black pepper. Pour and spread this over the meat to cover it. Sprinkle with the rest of the cheese, a little cinnamon, and a grinding of black pepper. Bake for 50 minutes–1 hour, until bubbling and golden.

6 Let the moussaka stand for 8–10 minutes, then sprinkle with some chopped parsley and cut into squares. Serve with a salad of tomato, red onion, and arugula.

Use lean ground beef to lower fat

•

Bulk out the ground beef with carrot

•

Reduce oil for frying eggplants by baking instead

•

Try a yogurt-base sauce instead of a white sauce

•

Up the meat sauce flavor with extra spices,
fresh herbs, and wine to reduce sodium

Fried fish and French fries with crushed peas

I was determined to make this popular fast-food dish healthier without compromising on taste and texture—especially because whenever I asked people why they liked it so much, the crisp, deep-fried batter always got a glowing mention. For this fresher version, both fish and fries are light and crisp without being at all greasy.

	Classic	Lighter
Kcals	915	649
Fat	36 g	27 g
Sat fat	11.5 g	4 g
Sodium	840 mg	348 mg

Per serving 649 kcals

Protein 41 g, carbohydrate 64 g, fat 27 g, saturated fat 4 g, fiber 7 g, sugar 4 g, sodium 348 mg

Serves 4

Prep: about 25 minutes
Cook: 40 minutes

For the French fries

7 equal-size russet potatoes, unpeeled

2 tablespoons olive oil

For the peas

2 cups frozen peas

1 tablespoon olive oil

2 teaspoons lemon juice

For the fish

4 (6 oz) pieces skinless haddock, halibut, hake, or cod fillet

⅓ cup all-purpose flour, plus 1 tablespoon

¼ teaspoon baking powder

⅓ cup cornstarch

1 large egg white

½ cup ice-cold sparkling water

2½ cups sunflower oil, for frying

1 lemon, cut into wedges

salt and freshly ground black pepper

1 Scrub the potatoes, cut them lengthwise into ½ inch-thick slices, then cut each slice into ½ inch-thick sticks. Put the potatoes into a large saucepan, pour in enough water to just cover, and bring to a boil, then lower the heat and gently simmer for 4 minutes. Drain, transfer to a clean dish towel, and pat dry, then let cool. This can be done 1–2 hours ahead.

2 Preheat the oven to 425°F. Put 1 tablespoon of the olive oil in a large, shallow nonstick roasting pan and heat in the oven for 10 minutes.

3 Transfer the potatoes to a bowl and toss in the remaining oil, using your hands. Spread out in a single layer in the hot roasting pan. Roast for 10 minutes, then turn them over. Roast for another 5 minutes, then turn again. Roast for a final 5–8 minutes, until crisp. Drain on paper towels.

4 While the fries are in the oven, cook the peas in boiling water for 4 minutes, then drain, put into the pan, and lightly crush with the back of a fork. Mix in the oil, lemon juice, and freshly ground black pepper. Cover and set aside.

5 The fish can also be cooked while the fries are in the oven. Pat the fillets dry with paper towels. Put the 1 tablespoon flour on a plate and use to coat each fillet, patting off the excess. Mix together the remaining flour, baking powder, cornstarch, a pinch of salt, and some black pepper. Lightly whisk the egg white with a wire whisk until frothy and bubbly but not too stiff. Pour the water into the flour mix, gently and briefly whisking as you work. The batter shouldn't be completely smooth. Add the egg white, then lightly whisk in just to mix. Try and keep as many bubbles as you can so that the batter stays light.

6 Pour the oil for frying into a heavy, medium nonstick wok or wok-shape pan. Preheat to 400°F; use a thermometer so that you can check the oil stays at that temperature. Cooking 2 pieces of fish at a time, dip them in the batter to coat and let some of it drip off, then lower into the hot oil using a slotted spoon. Fry for 5–6 minutes, making sure the oil stays at 400°F and turning the fish over halfway through so that it is golden all over. Lift out with a slotted spoon, drain on paper towels, and keep hot. Check the oil temperature is 400°F, then repeat with the remaining fish. Reheat the peas and serve with the fish, fries, and lemon wedges.

keep the skin on potatoes to increase the fiber content

•

cut fat fries and oven roast them to reduce fat

•

use a nonstick wok for frying the fish,
and thoroughly drain the cooked fish and fries

•

make a fat-free, tempura-style batter

•

serve with peas and lemon to boost vitamin c

Fish cakes

Creating a golden crispy coating for a fish cake is hard to achieve without using a lot of butter or oil to fry it in. By changing the cooking method and using the oven instead of the skillet, this recipe has been transformed into a healthy low-fat dinner with a lot of crunch appeal.

	Classic	Lighter
Kcals	370	239
Fat	17.9 g	5 g
Sat fat	4.6 g	0.6 g
Sodium	760 mg	280 mg

Per serving 239 kcals

Protein 25.8 g, carbs 22.6 g, fat 5.0 g, sat fat 0.6 g, fiber 1.9 g, sugar 0.9 g, sodium 280 mg

Makes 4

Prep: 35 minutes, plus cooling and chilling
Cook: 30 minutes

1 lb skinless haddock or halibut fillet

1 tablespoon canola oil, plus extra for greasing

2 large russet or Yukon gold potatoes, chopped into 1½ inch chunks

1 tablespoon chopped parsley

2 tablespoons snipped chives

½ teaspoon finely grated lemon zest

1 teaspoon drained capers, finely chopped

½ teaspoon Dijon mustard

1 large egg

1 cup fresh white bread crumbs

1½ teaspoons all-purpose flour, for shaping

salt and freshly ground black pepper

lemon wedges to serve

1 Preheat the oven to 400°F. Lightly brush the center of a large piece of aluminum foil with a little canola oil. Lay the fish on the oiled foil, season with black pepper, then wrap it up and seal to make a package. Place on a baking sheet and bake for 12–15 minutes or until just cooked. Unwrap the package and set aside to cool.

2 While the fish is baking, cook the potatoes in boiling water for 10–12 minutes or until tender. Drain, return to the dry pan, and let them dry out for 1 minute on low heat, then remove and mash with a fork. Mix in the parsley, chives, lemon zest, capers, and mustard, then season with black pepper and a pinch of salt.

3 Drain the fish from its package, then flake it into big chunks. Gently stir the fish into the potato without breaking it up. Set aside to cool.

4 Beat the egg on a large plate and spread the bread crumbs on another plate. Divide the fish cake mixture into 4. On a lightly floured surface or board, shape the mixture into 4 circles, about 1 inch thick. Dip each cake in the egg to coat, then cover all over with the bread crumbs. Pat to reshape and chill for 20 minutes, or overnight.

5 Heat the oven to 375°F. For each fish cake, spoon ½ teaspoon of the oil in a circle on a nonstick baking pan (with sides to contain the oil when cooking). Sit each fish cake on a circle of oil and drizzle ¼ teaspoon oil over the top of each one. Bake for 10 minutes, then turn each one over once golden and bake for another 5–8 minutes, until also golden underneath.

oven bake the fish cakes instead of frying to lower the fat, and use a nonstick baking pan so that minimum oil is needed

Quiche Lorraine

Butter, cream, bacon, eggs, and yolks are all high in fat and the crisp, flaky pastry is key to this recipe. However, there are ways of balancing the right kinds of fats to achieve a great-tasting lighter quiche.

	Classic	Lighter
Kcals	525	272
Fat	45 g	17 g
Sat fat	25 g	6 g
Sodium	484 mg	368 mg

Per serving 272 kcals

Protein 13 g, carbs 19 g, fat 17 g, sat fat 6 g, fiber 1 g, sugar 2 g, sodium 368 mg

Serves 8

Prep: 35 minutes plus chilling
Cook: 45–55 minutes

For the pastry dough

1⅓ cups all-purpose flour, plus extra for dusting

⅓ cup plus 1 teaspoon Greek yogurt

¼ cup extra virgin olive oil

1 garlic clove, finely crushed

For the filling

6 oz lean, sliced good-quality ham, trimmed of all fat and cut ½ inch thick

2 oz Gruyère cheese

3 extra-large eggs

1 cup reduced-fat crème fraîche or light cream

½ cup whole milk

good pinch of ground or freshly grated nutmeg, plus extra for sprinkling

salt and freshly ground black pepper

1 For the pastry dough, put the flour into a bowl with the yogurt, olive oil, garlic, a pinch of salt, and a generous grinding of black pepper. Using a blunt knife, mix to a dough, then briefly knead until smooth.

2 Roll the dough out on a lightly floured surface as thinly as you can, then use it to line a 9 inch-round, 1 inch-deep, loose-bottom, fluted tart pan. Trim the dough edges with scissors so that the dough sits slightly above the pan, then wrap and reserve the scraps. Press the dough into the flutes of the pan. Lightly prick the bottom with a fork and chill for 10 minutes. Preheat the oven to 400°F and in a baking sheet to heat.

3 Line the pastry bottom with aluminum foil, shiny side down, fill with dried beans, then bake on the hot baking sheet for 15 minutes. Remove the foil and beans, then bake for 5–7 minutes or until the pastry is slightly golden all over and no longer raw on the bottom. Remove from the oven and, if any small cracks appear in the pastry, patch them with the reserved pastry scraps.

4 Meanwhile, prepare the filling. Cut the ham into cubes. Cut half of the cheese into cubes and finely grate the rest. Beat the eggs with a fork, then beat in the crème fraîche, followed by the milk. Season with nutmeg and black pepper.

5 Spread the ham and cheese over the cooked pastry bottom. Pour the egg mixture over the ham and cheese, then sprinkle with a little more nutmeg. Put the tart into the oven, then lower the heat to 375°F. Bake for 25–30 minutes or until softly set and tinged golden. Let settle for 5 minutes before removing from the pan. Serve while warm and softly set—it's also good cold.

Use olive oil and Greek yogurt instead of butter and egg yolks to make the dough

Chicken korma

My challenge with this recipe was to create creaminess without cream, but also to delve into its heritage to find authentic ways to lighten yet enrich. Spicy and aromatic, it's definitely a healthy alternative.

	Classic	Lighter
Kcals	613	402
Fat	34 g	12 g
Sat fat	20 g	3 g
Sodium	168 mg	140 mg

Per serving 402 kcals

Protein 43 g, carbs 33 g, fat 12 g, sat fat 3 g, fiber 1 g, sugar 7 g, sodium 140 mg

Serves 4

Prep: 15 minutes
Cook: 45 minutes

2 tablespoons vegetable oil

2 medium onions, chopped

5 cardamom pods

3 garlic cloves, finely chopped

(1 inch piece fresh ginger root, peeled and finely chopped

1 cinnamon stick

1 lb 5 oz boneless, skinless chicken breasts, cut into bite-size pieces

2 teaspoons ground coriander

1½ teaspoons garam masala

¼ teaspoon ground mace

¼ teaspoon ground black pepper

⅔ cup plain yogurt, at room temperature

½ cup whole milk

2 small green chiles, seeded and shredded

handful of fresh cilantro leaves and stems, coarsely chopped

1 tablespoon slivered almonds, toasted

salt

2 cups basmati or other long-grain rice, cooked with a pinch of saffron threads, to serve

1 Heat 1 tablespoon of the oil in a deep sauté pan. Add the onions, then sauté over medium-high heat for 12–15 minutes, stirring occasionally, until a rich golden color. Meanwhile, make a slit down the length of each cardamom pod just deep enough to reveal the seeds. Remove the onions from the heat. Transfer one-third of them to a mini blender along with the garlic, ginger, and 2 tablespoons water. Blend together to make a smooth paste. Set aside.

2 Return the onions in the pan to the heat, add the remaining oil, the cardamom pods, and cinnamon stick, then stir-fry for 2 minutes. Stir in the chicken, ground coriander, 1¼ teaspoons of the garam masala, the mace and black pepper, then stir-fry for another 2 minutes. Reserve 3 tablespoons of the yogurt, then slowly add the rest, 1 tablespoon at a time, stirring between each spoonful.

3 Stir the onion paste into the mixture and stir-fry for 2–3 minutes. Stir in ⅔ cup water, then the milk. Bring to a boil, then simmer, covered, for 20 minutes, sprinkling in the chiles for the final 5 minutes. Remove the cardamom pods and cinnamon stick. The flavors mellow all the more if refrigerated overnight. When gently reheating, splash in a little water, if needed, to thin the korma sauce.

4 Finish by stirring in the chopped fresh cilantro. Taste and add a little salt, if desired. Swirl in the reserved yogurt. Spoon the korma into bowls, then sprinkle a few toasted almonds over each portion with a sprinkling of the remaining garam masala. Serve with the saffron rice on the side.

Replace cream or coconut milk with milk and yogurt to reduce fat

Lasagna

Traditionally, lasagna was made for special occasions and can be very rich. The pasta should be rolled out thinly to create fine layers—this speedier version has fewer layers of pasta for a similar light effect.

	Classic	Lighter
Kcals	770	447
Fat	50 g	19 g
Sat fat	26 g	9 g
Sodium	796 mg	384 mg

Per serving 447 kcals

Protein 38 g, carbs 31 g, fat 19 g, sat fat 9 g, fiber 4 g, sugar 9 g, sodium 384 mg

Serves 6

Prep: 35–40 minutes
Cook: 1 hour 50 minutes

For the meat sauce

1 tablespoon olive oil

1 onion, chopped

2 medium carrots, diced

3 plump garlic cloves, finely chopped

9 oz lean top sirloin steak, trimmed of all fat, thinly sliced, then ground

9 oz lean ground pork

½ cup red wine

2 tablespoons tomato paste

1 (14½ oz) can plum tomatoes

½ teaspoon ground nutmeg, plus a pinch

handful of basil leaves, torn

For the other layers

1 (10 oz) package spinach leaves

1 large egg

1 cup ricotta cheese

handful of flat leaf parsley leaves, chopped

6 wide oven-ready lasagna noodles (about 6 oz)

4 ½ oz mozzarella, preferably buffalo, coarsely chopped

½ cup coarsely grated Parmesan cheese

8–12 cherry tomatoes on the vine

salt and freshly ground black pepper

basil leaves and salad greens, to serve

1 Make the meat sauce. Heat the oil in a large sauté pan, then add the onion and sauté for 5 minutes, until golden brown. Add the carrots and garlic and sauté for another 2 minutes. Stir in both meats, breaking up the pork with a wooden spoon. Cook over high heat until the meat is no longer pink and the juices are released. Pour in the wine, scrape the bottom of the pan as you stir, then cook for 1–2 minutes, until the liquid is reduced.

2 Next, add the tomato paste, tomatoes, and 2 tablespoons of water, then stir to break up tomatoes. Add ½ teaspoon nutmeg and some black pepper, cover, then simmer for 1 hour, stirring occasionally. Taste, season with salt if necessary, and stir in the torn basil. The sauce can be chilled for up to 1 day at this stage.

3 Meanwhile, prepare the other layers. Put the spinach into a large bowl and pour boiling water over the leaves. After 30 seconds, put the spinach into a colander and put under cold running water briefly to cool. Squeeze to remove excess water. Beat the egg in a bowl, then mix with the ricotta, parsley, the pinch of nutmeg, and black pepper.

4 Soak the lasagna noodles in a single layer in boiling water for 5 minutes. (Although oven-ready noodles, I find soaking improves the texture.) Drain well. Preheat the oven to 400°F.

5 Spread a few big spoonfuls of sauce to barely cover the bottom of an 8 x 11 inch ovenproof dish. Cover with 2 lasagna noodles, then spread half the remaining sauce over them. Cover with another 2 lasagna noodles, then spread the spinach evenly over the noodles. Spread the ricotta mixture on top and cover with 2 more lasagna noodles. Spread with the remaining sauce, then sprinkle with the mozzarella and Parmesan to almost cover the meat. Top with the cherry tomatoes and some black pepper, then cover loosely with aluminum foil.

6 Bake for 35 minutes, then remove the foil and bake for another 5–10 minutes. Let stand for a few minutes, then sprinkle with basil and serve with salad.

OTHER WAYS TO USE ...

The meat sauce
Serve as a meat sauce over spaghetti or tagliatelle.

Replace ground beef with lean ground pork and top sirloin steak and use less oil to reduce fat

•

Use spinach as one of the lasagna layers

•

Boost veg by mixing carrots into a meat sauce and topping with tomatoes

Pork stir-fry

Perfect for when there's just the two of you, a stir-fry is one of the fastest dinners to cook. Choosing the cut of meat wisely helps lower the fat—but there can still be a danger from it being high in salt if too much soy sauce is splashed in. I've found several ways to trim the fat and sodium, so they have been dramatically reduced, but you won't miss out on flavor.

	Classic	Lighter
Kcals	348	230
Fat	22.7 g	8.8 g
Sat fat	6.5 g	1.8 g
Sodium	1,640 mg	520 mg

Per serving 230 kcals

Protein 31.8 g, carbs 6 g, fat 8.8 g, sat fat 1.8 g, fiber 3.4 g, sugar 2.9 g, sodium 520 mg

Serves 2

Prep: 25 minutes
Cook: 10 minutes

1 teaspoon rice wine or dry sherry

1 tablespoon dark soy sauce

½ teaspoon Chinese five-spice powder

1 teaspoon cornstarch

9 oz pork tenderloin, trimmed of all fat, cut into thin, 2–3 inch-long slices

5 scallions, ends trimmed

6 asparagus spears, trimmed

4 oz bok choy

3 oz baby broccoli spears

1 teaspoon peanut oil

2 teaspoons finely chopped fresh ginger root

2 garlic cloves, finely chopped

½ teaspoon sesame oil

1 teaspoon toasted sesame seeds

freshly ground black pepper

1 Mix together the rice wine or sherry, soy sauce, five-spice, cornstarch, and a grinding of black pepper in a shallow dish. Toss in the pork to coat it, cover, and let marinate while you prepare the vegetables.

2 Slice the scallions and asparagus diagonally into 2 inch pieces. Slice the bok choy into 1 inch pieces and the broccoli spears into 2 inch pieces. Steam the asparagus and broccoli for 2 minutes, lay the bok choy on top, and steam for another 1–1½ minutes so that it still has some bite to it. Remove from the steamer.

3 Heat a wok or large skillet, preferably nonstick. Pour in the peanut oil and, when it is hot, add the pork and stir-fry for 2 minutes or until almost cooked and turning brown. Add the scallions, ginger, and garlic and stir-fry for another 2 minutes. Stir in enough water to make it a little saucy, about ½ cup, then mix in the steamed vegetables to quickly warm through. For more sauce, pour in a splash more water. Serve drizzled with the sesame oil and sprinkled with the sesame seeds.

Reduce sodium by using less soy sauce and adding five-spice powder to maintain flavor; use dark soy sauce for a more intense taste and bulk it out with water

Steak and kidney pie

Everyone enjoys the meat and gravy in this dish and the pastry needs to be generous and gusty, so this is a healthier pie that is still rich, desirable, and hearty.

	Classic	Lighter
Kcals	683	373
Fat	41 g	14 g
Sat fat	22 g	5 g
Sodium	488 mg	168 mg

Per serving 373 kcals

Protein 33 g, carbs 28 g, fat 14 g, sat fat 5 g, fiber 3 g, sugar 7 g, sodium 168 ,g

Serves 6

Prep: 30 minutes
Cook: 2¼ hours

For the filling

7 oz kidneys, halved

1 tablespoon canola oil

2 onions, chopped

2 bay leaves

4 sprigs of thyme

1¼ lb lean beef round or boneless beef chuck, cut into chunks

½ cup red wine

2 teaspoons tomato paste

1 teaspoon dry English mustard

2 tablespoons all-purpose flour

1 large carrot, chopped

4 flat mushrooms, thickly sliced

6 oz cremini mushrooms, quartered or halved if small

3 tablespoons chopped parsley

For the pastry dough

1¼ cups all-purpose flour, plus extra for dusting

1 teaspoon thyme leaves (optional)

1 tablespoon cold (or frozen) butter

¼ cup reduced-fat Greek yogurt

2 tablespoons extra virgin olive oil

salt and freshly ground black pepper

1   Cut out and discard the thin tubes from the kidneys. Rinse the kidneys in cold water until the water runs clear, pat dry, then chop them into small pieces. Heat the oil in a large saucepan or deep sauté pan. Add the onions, bay leaves, and sprigs of thyme and cook over medium heat for 8–10 minutes, until the onions are golden brown, stirring often. Fill the kettle or a saucepan of water and put it on the stove to boil.

2   Add the steak and kidney to the pan and stir-fry briefly, just until they lose their pink color. Increase the heat, pour in the wine, and stir to deglaze the bottom of the pan, then let it boil over a high heat for 2–3 minutes, until reduced and absorbed into the meat. Stir in the tomato paste and dry mustard. Sift in the flour, stirring, then stir for a couple of minutes.

3 Pour in 1¾ cups of boiling water and continue stirring until the mixture starts to boil and is thickened. Add the carrot and both mushrooms, reduce the heat, and cover with a lid, then let simmer gently for about 1 hour, stirring occasionally. Remove the lid and simmer for another 25–30 minutes or until the meat is tender and the gravy has thickened slightly.

4 Remove the pan from the heat and remove the bay leaves and sprigs of thyme. Stir in the parsley, season to taste, then transfer to a 9 inch round pie or ovenproof dish and let cool slightly. Preheat the oven to 400°F).

5 While the meat is cooling, make the pastry dough. Put the flour, and thyme if using, into a bowl. Grate in the cold or frozen butter, make a well in the center, then add the yogurt, olive oil, a pinch of salt, and a good grinding of black pepper. Using a blunt knife, mix together with 2 teaspoons cold water, then gently gather together with your hands to form a dough. Remove from the bowl and knead briefly until smooth.

6 Roll out the dough on a lightly floured surface until it's slightly bigger than the top of the pie dish. Lay the pastry over the meat and trim the edges so that it slightly overhangs the edges of the dish. Make 2 small slits in the center. Flute the edges, then roll out the scraps and cut out 6 diamond-shape leaves. Dampen one side and lay them on the pastry lid. Place the dish on a baking sheet, then bake in the oven for about 25 minutes or until the pastry is golden.

use lean beef round—and less of it—to lower fat

•

make a shortcrust pastry with minimum butter, adding olive oil and yogurt instead

•

use water instead of stock for gravy and bump up the flavor with herbs, wine, tomato paste, and dry mustard to reduce salt

•

increase veg by adding mushrooms and carrots

Crispy chicken

If you love takeout chicken, you will be amazed by this low-fat version. The chicken is only fried briefly and then cooked in the oven, greatly reducing the amount of fat. The longer you leave the chicken pieces in the buttermilk marinade, the more tender and juicy they will be. The crispy chicken pieces are delicious served with crunchy coleslaw.

	Classic	Lighter
Kcals	412	319
Fat	22.7 g	10.5 g
Sat fat	6 g	1.1 g
Sodium	1,400 mg	280 mg

Per serving 319 kcals

Protein 37.1 g, carbs 18.6 g, fat 10.5 g, sat fat 1.1 g, fiber 0.8 g, sugar 2.2 g, sodium 280 mg

Serves 4

Prep: 15 minutes, plus marinating
Cook: 25 minutes

⅔ cup buttermilk

2 plump garlic cloves, crushed

4 (5 oz) boneless, skinless chicken breasts

½ cup Japanese panko bread crumbs

2 tablespoons all-purpose flour

pinch of baking powder

½ rounded teaspoon paprika

¼ rounded teaspoon dry English mustard

¼ rounded teaspoon dried thyme

¼ teaspoon hot chili powder

½ teaspoon ground black pepper

pinch of fine sea salt

3 tablespoons canola oil

Crunchy Coleslaw (see p. 63), to serve

1 To prepare the marinade, pour the buttermilk into a wide, shallow dish and stir in the garlic. Slice the chicken into chunky slices, about 3¾ inches long and 1¼–1½ inches wide. Lay the chicken in the dish and turn it over in the buttermilk so that it is well coated. Cover and let rest in the refrigerator for 1–2 hours, or preferably overnight.

2 To prepare the coating for the chicken, heat a large, nonstick skillet and add the panko crumbs, flour, and baking powder. Toast them in the pan for 2–3 minutes, stirring regularly so that they brown evenly and don't burn. Transfer the crumb mix to a bowl and stir in the paprika, mustard, thyme, chili powder, black pepper, and sea salt. Set aside.

3 When you are ready to cook the chicken, preheat the oven to 450°F. Line a baking pan with aluminum foil and sit a wire rack (preferably nonstick) on top. Transfer half the crumb mix to a medium-large plastic bag. Lift half the chicken from the buttermilk, leaving the marinade clinging to it. Transfer it to the bag of seasoned crumbs. Seal the end of the bag and give it a good shake so that the chicken gets well covered (you could do all the crumbs and chicken together if you prefer, but it's easier to coat it evenly in 2 batches).

4 Remove the chicken from the bag. Heat 1 tablespoon of the oil in a large, nonstick skillet, then add the chicken pieces and cook for 1½ minutes without moving them. Turn the chicken over, pour in another ½ tablespoon of the oil to cover the bottom of the pan, and cook for another 1 minute, so that both sides are becoming golden brown. Using tongs, transfer to the wire rack. Repeat with the remaining seasoned crumbs, oil, and chicken.

5 Bake all the chicken on the rack for 15 minutes, until cooked and crisp. Serve with Crunchy Coleslaw (see opposite).

To provide a low-fat coating for the crumb mix
to stick to, use buttermilk

•

Use Panko bread crumbs—Japanese dried bread flakes.
When fried, they absorb less fat than regular bread crumbs
and stay light and crisp once cooked

Crunchy coleslaw

Coleslaw salad is a traditional accompaniment to takeout fried chicken, but usually not much better for you. This version still has creaminess and crunch, but without all the mayonnaise.

	Classic	Lighter
Kcals	189	123
Fat	17.3 g	7.2 g
Sat fat	2.6 g	1.6 g
Sodium	600 mg	160 mg

Per serving 123 kcals

Protein 4.1 g, carbs 10.1 g, fat 7.2 g, sat fat 1.6 g, fiber 4.7 g, sugar 8.7 g, 160 mg

Serves 4

Prep: 20 minutes, plus chilling and standing (optional)

½ head of green cabbage

3 carrots, shredded

6 scallions, ends trimmed and chopped

2 teaspoons canola oil

2 teaspoons white wine vinegar

2 teaspoons whole-grain mustard

2 tablespoons plain yogurt

2 tablespoons reduced-fat crème fraîche or Greek yogurt

2 tablespoons orange juice

2 tablespoons sunflower seeds, toasted

salt and freshly ground black pepper

1 To make the coleslaw, cut out and discard the hard core from the cabbage, then finely shred the leaves. Put into a bowl with the carrots and scallions and mix well. Season with black pepper and a pinch of salt, then cover and chill for 1–2 hours (optional).

2 Mix together the oil, vinegar, and mustard in a small bowl, then stir in the yogurt, crème fraîche, and orange juice. Set aside.

3 When ready to serve, pour the dressing over the vegetables, add the sunflower seeds, and toss together. Let the coleslaw sit for 10–15 minutes so the flavors can blend.

Toasting seeds and adding mustard to the coleslaw dressing gives extra flavor, so you need less salt

Macaroni and cheese

Making macaroni and cheese can be a juggling act, so it's easier if you get a few things prepared ahead. I've found new ways to lighten this dish so it has half the fat but all the flavor.

	Classic	Lighter
Kcals	821	503
Fat	43 g	19 g
Sat fat	26 g	11 g
Sodium	792 mg	460 mg

Per serving 503 kcals

Protein 26 g, carbs 62 g, fat 19 g, sat fat 11 g, fiber 3 g, sugar 14 g, sodium 460 mg.

Serves 4

Prep: 30 minutes
Cook: 35 minutes

2⅓ cups low-fat milk

3 tablespoons cornstarch

1 heaping teaspoon dry English mustard

1 large garlic clove, finely chopped

generous pinch of crushed dried red pepper flakes

5 oz extra sharp cheddar cheese

1 oz Parmesan cheese

½ cup fresh bread crumbs

1 lb mixture of tomatoes, such as cherry and medium sizes

1 bunch scallions, ends trimmed

8 oz macaroni

⅔ cup buttermilk

salt and freshly ground black pepper

1 Mix 3 tablespoons of the milk with the cornstarch and mustard, and set aside. Heat the rest of the milk with the garlic until just coming to a boil. Remove from the heat, sprinkle in the red pepper flakes, and let steep while you get everything else ready.

2 Coarsely s both cheeses, keeping them separate. Mix a handful of the cheddar into the bread crumbs with a grinding of black pepper. Thickly slice the medium tomatoes and halve the cherry. Finely slice the scallions. Preheat the oven to 375°F.

3 Bring a saucepan of water to a boil, add the macaroni, give it a stir so that it doesn't stick, and then cook for 6 minutes, stirring occasionally. Stir in the scallions and cook for another 2 minutes. Meanwhile, make the sauce. Stir the cornstarch mix into the warm milk. Return the pan to the heat, then bring to a boil, stirring, until thickened and smooth. Remove from the heat and stir in the Parmesan, most of the remaining cheddar, and some black pepper to taste. Stir in the buttermilk.

4 Transfer the macaroni to a colander, drain, then hold under hot running water to keep it all separate. Drain well, then stir into the sauce. Pour into an ovenproof dish, about 12 x 8 inches. Lay the tomatoes over the top, then sprinkle with the cheesy bread crumbs, the rest of the cheese, and a grating of black pepper. Bake for about 15 minutes, until starting to bubble around the edges. Broil for about 5 minutes, until the top is crisp and well browned. Let sit for a few minutes to settle before serving.

Reduce the fat by making a butterless sauce, using less of an extra sharp cheese combined with Parmesan to maintain flavor, and substituting some of the milk for low-fat buttermilk

Chicken pie

It's hard to resist the temptation of a classic chicken pie, with its creamy filling and crisp, buttery flaky or puff pastry topping. This recipe has rich, comforting qualities, too—but in a much healthier way.

	Classic	Lighter
Kcals	794	320
Fat	51.3 g	10.4 g
Sat fat	29.3 g	3.6 g
Sodium	860 mg	548 mg

Per serving 320 kcals

Protein 34 g, carbs 22 g, fat 10 g, sat fat 4 g, fiber 3g, sugar 7 g, sodium 548 mg

Serves 4

Prep: 30 minutes, plus cooling
Cook: 45–50 minutes

For the filling

2 cups chicken stock, from a bouillon cube

½ cup dry white wine

2 garlic cloves, finely chopped

3 sprigs of thyme

1 sprig tarragon, plus 1 tablespoon chopped tarragon leaves

4 carrots, cut into batons

4 (5 oz) boneless, skinless chicken breasts

2 leeks, trimmed, cleaned, and sliced

2 tablespoons cornstarch mixed with 2 tablespoons water

3 tablespoons crème fraîche or reduced-fat light cream

1 heaped teaspoon Dijon mustard

1 heaped tablespoon chopped flat leaf or curly parsley

For the topping

3 sheets phyllo pastry, each about 15 x 12 inches, about 2½ oz total weight

1 tablespoon canola oil

freshly ground black pepper

1 Pour the stock and wine into a large, wide skillet. Add the garlic, thyme, tarragon sprig, and carrots, bring to a boil, then lower the heat and simmer for 3 minutes. Lay the chicken in the stock, grind over some black pepper, cover, and simmer for 5 minutes. Spread the leek slices over the chicken, replace the lid, then gently simmer for another 10 minutes, so that the leeks steam while the chicken cooks. Remove from the heat and let the chicken sit in the stock for about 15 minutes to keep it moist while cooling slightly.

2 Strain the stock into a liquid measuring cup—you should have 2 cups; if not, make up with water. Transfer the chicken and vegetables to a 1½ quart pie dish and discard the herb sprigs.

3 Pour the stock back into the skillet, then slowly pour in the cornstarch mixture. Return the pan to the heat and bring to a boil, stirring constantly, until thickened. Remove from the heat and stir in the crème fraîche, mustard, chopped tarragon, and parsley. Season with black pepper. Preheat the oven to 400°F.

4 Tear or cut the chicken into chunky shreds. Pour the sauce over the chicken mixture, then stir everything together.

5 Cut each sheet of phyllo into 4 squares or rectangles. Layer them on top of the filling, brushing each sheet with some of the oil as you work. Lightly scrunch up the phyllo so that it doesn't lie completely flat ,and tuck the edges into the sides of the dish or lay them on the edges if the dish has a rim. Grind over a little black pepper, place the dish on a baking sheet, then bake for 20–25 minutes, until golden and the sauce is bubbling. Serve immediately.

OTHER WAYS TO USE …

The filling
Serve minus the pastry lid with boiled rice instead, or toss with cooked pasta for a family-friendly dinner.

The phyllo pastry topping
Use to cover a fish casserole, or apple or other fruit pie, instead of high-fat puff or flaky pastry.

Use skinless chicken breasts instead of thighs to reduce fat

•

Boost flavor by poaching chicken in stock and a little wine, with some garlic and herbs

•

Pack in as many vegetables as possible

•

Blend cornstarch into the flavored stock to make and thicken the sauce. For a rich creaminess, replace heavy cream with some crème fraîche

Shepherd's pie

Traditional shepherd's pie uses ground lamb, which means it is slightly high in fat, so this recipe uses the leanest I could find. Substituting some of the meat for lentils really transforms this recipe.

	Classic	Lighter
Kcals	666	429
Fat	38 g	12 g
Sat fat	20 g	4 g
Sodium	400 mg	364 mg

Per serving 429 kcals

Protein 22 g, carbs 63 g, fat 12 g, sat fat 4 g, fiber 11 g, sugar 15 g, sodium 346 mg

Serves 4

Prep: 25 minutes
Cook: 1 hour 25–30 minutes

For the filling

1 tablespoon canola oil

1 onion, chopped

3–4 sprigs of thyme

2 cups diced carrots

9 oz lean ground lamb

1 tablespoon all-purpose flour

1 teaspoon vegetable bouillon, made up to 1½ cups stock with boiling water

1 cup canned diced tomatoes

1 tablespoon tomato paste

2 cups canned green lentils, with no added sodium, or cooked green lentils, drained

1 teaspoon Worcestershire sauce

For the topping

6 russet or Yukon gold potatoes, coarsely chopped

1 large sweet potato, coarsely chopped

2 tablespoons reduced-fat crème fraîche or Greek yogurt

1 tablespoon low-fat milk

freshly ground black pepper

1 Heat the oil in a large, deep sauté pan or saucepan. Add the onion and sprigs of thyme and sauté for 2–3 minutes. Then add the carrots and sauté together for 5–8 minutes, stirring occasionally until the vegetables start to brown. Stir in the ground lamb to break it down. Cook for 1–2 minutes, until no longer pink. Stir in the flour, scraping the bottom of the pan in case the meat sticks, then cook for another 1–2 minutes. Pour in the stock and stir until thickened. Stir in the tomatoes, tomato paste, lentils, and Worcestershire sauce and season with black pepper. Reduce the heat and simmer, covered, for 45 minutes, stirring occasionally.

2 Meanwhile, prepare the topping. Put all the chopped potatoes into a large saucepan of boiling water. Bring back to a boil, then simmer for 12–15 minutes or until the potatoes are tender. Drain well in a colander, then transfer back into the pan. Mash with a masher or, briefly, with an electric hand mixer until smooth. Beat in the crème fraîche and milk with a wooden spoon until light and fluffy. Preheat the oven to 400°F.

3 Spoon the meat into a 1½ quart pie dish and remove the sprigs of thyme. Top with the mashed potatoes and smooth over with a knife. Use a fork to create a ridged pattern on top. Place the dish on a baking sheet and bake for 20–25 minutes, until piping hot and the filling starts to bubble around the edges. If the top is not brown enough, put it under a hot broiler for 5 minutes or so until the mash is crisp and golden. Let it sit for 5 minutes, then serve.

use lean ground meat to reduce fat and canola oil to reduce saturated fat

Pizza Margherita

As with many things that have a bread base, it's what you sprinkle on to a pizza that can pile on the fat, especially saturated fat. Even with the simple, classic Margherita, the main fat culprit is cheese. With less kneading required (thanks to a method food writer Dan Lepard showed me) and a few easy tweaks, this pizza is lower in fat and sodium, but still big on flavor.

	Classic	Lighter
Kcals	601	498
Fat	23.3 g	13.5 g
Sat fat	12 g	6.6 g
Sodium	1,120 mg	680 mg

Per serving 498 kcals

Protein 19.6 g, carbs 73.7 g, fat 13.5 g, sat fat 6.6 g, fiber 3.9 g, sugar 5.6 g, sodium 680 mg

Makes 2 (each pizza serves 2)

Prep: 20 minutes, plus rising and resting
Cook: 15 minutes per pizza

For the dough

2½ cups white bread flour, plus extra for dusting

⅓ cup plus semolina, preferably coarse, plus 4 teaspoons

1 teaspoon salt

2¼ teaspoons active dry yeast

3 teaspoons olive oil

For the topping

1 (14½ oz) can plum tomatoes

3 garlic cloves, finely chopped

1 tablespoon tomato paste

2 handfuls basil leaves

2 oz mozzarella cheese

¾ cup ricotta cheese

12 cherry tomatoes, halved

(1 cup arugula leaves

2 tablespoons grated fresh Parmesan cheese

salt and freshly ground black pepper

1 Combine the flour, ⅓ cup plus 1 tablespoon of the semolina, the salt, and yeast in a large mixing bowl. Pour in 2 teaspoons of the oil and 1 cup of water and mix together with your hands, adding another 3 tablespoons of water to pick up any dry parts in the bottom of the bowl, if needed. The dough should feel sticky. Once it is mixed, cover and let stand for 15 minutes.

2 Transfer the dough to a lightly floured surface and knead for just 12 times. Shape it into a ball and return it to the bowl. Cover and let stand for 10 minutes. Repeat the kneading and letting stand for 10 minutes. Then, knead one more time and let stand for 15 minutes.

3 While the dough is resting, prepare the topping. Put the can of tomatoes into a strainer set over a bowl to drain off the juices. Put the tomatoes in a bowl and snip them into small pieces, using scissors. Stir in the garlic and tomato paste with some black pepper and a pinch of salt. Set aside. Line a baking sheet with parchment paper and sprinkle with ½ teaspoon of the remaining semolina. Preheat the oven to 475°F.

4 Cut the dough in half. Keep one half in the bowl and knead the other half just a few times on a lightly floured surface. Roll out to an 11 inch circle, pulling it into shape as well as rolling if that is easier. If the dough is sticking while rolling out, rub just a little of the remaining oil on the work surface to help it grip. Lift it on to the baking sheet, draped over a rolling pin if that works better.

5 Spread half of the tomato sauce over the dough, almost to the edge. Sprinkle over one handful of the basil in torn pieces. Tear half of the mozzarella and spread that over teh sauce, then dot small spoonfuls of the ricotta all over the dough. Sprinkle over half of the cherry tomatoes and season with black pepper. Bake for 15 minutes, until the dough is golden and crisp and the topping is bubbling. Repeat with the other half of the dough and toppings. Serve each pizza sprinkled with half of the arugula and Parmesan with a drizzle of the remaining oil over each (about ½ teaspoon over each).

TIPS

- Sodium has been slightly reduced in the dough, but it's worth noting that if you reduce it too much, your dough will be less lively, because a certain amount is necessary to create a good texture and stop it from being slack.

- Semolina is added to give the dough authenticity and to enrich and strengthen it.

- If you want to increase the fiber in the dough, replace ¾ cup of the white bread flour with whole-wheat bread flour.

make a no-cook tomato sauce to eliminate oil for cooking

•

Sprinkle extra fresh tomatoes and arugula on top to add to your five a day

•

Lower the fat by replacing some of the mozzarella with ricotta cheese

•

Bake on a baking sheet lined with parchment paper, so there's no need to oil it

Burgers with roasted pepper salsa

Burgers can be high in fat and calories, but it's not just the meat that's to blame. It's the little extras we pile on top—the cheese, ketchup, and mayonnaise. This recipe lightens the load but not the burger experience.

	Classic	Lighter
Kcals	604	405
Fat	39.7 g	15.4 g
Sat fat	12.7 g	5 g
Sodium	800 mg	576 mg

Per serving 405 kcals

Protein 32 g, carbs 37 g, fat 15.4 g, sat fat 5 g, fiber 5 g, sugar 10 g, sodium 576 g

Serves 4

Prep: 25 minutes, plus chilling and cooling
Cook: 45–50 minutes

For the burgers

14 oz lean ground beef

5 scallions, ends trimmed and finely chopped

2 carrots, finely shredded

2 garlic cloves, finely chopped

2 teaspoons Dijon mustard

1 tablespoon chopped tarragon

1 large egg, beaten

4 whole-wheat bread rolls, halved

1½ teaspoons canola oil

1 cup watercress or salad greens

For the roasted pepper salsa

2 large red bell peppers, halved lengthwise, cored, and seeded

6 cherry or baby plum tomatoes, halved

2 teaspoons lime juice

2 teaspoons snipped chives

¼ small red onion, thinly sliced

pinch of crushed dried red pepper flakes

salt and freshly ground black pepper

1 Put the ground beef into a bowl with the scallions, shredded carrot, garlic, mustard, tarragon, and egg. Mix well using a fork. Season with black pepper and a pinch of salt, then divide the mixture equally into 4. Flatten each piece with your hands into a 4 inch circle, about ¾ inch thick. Chill for about 30 minutes. Alternatively, the burgers can be made a day ahead; stack the burgers between pieces of wax paper to stop them from sticking, wrap in plastic wrap, then chill until ready to cook.

2 Meanwhile, preheat the oven to 400°F. Lay the bell peppers, cut sides down, on a nonstick baking sheet. Roast for 35 minutes, until the skins are charred, laying the tomatoes next to them, cut side up, for the final 3 minutes just to soften slightly. Remove and immediately transfer the bell peppers to a small bowl, then cover with plastic wrap. Let stand for 5–10 minutes, until cool enough to handle.

3 To make the salsa, peel off the bell pepper skins, chop the bell peppers, and add them back into the bowl to join any juices there. Chop the tomatoes and stir into the bell peppers with the lime juice, chives, onion, and red pepper flakes. Taste and season with black pepper, if necessary. Set aside. The salsa can be made 1–2 days ahead and chilled.

4 Heat a ridged grill pan, or cook the burgers on the barbecue. Lay the cut sides of the buns on the grill and cook until marked with grill lines. Brush each burger on one side with some of the canola oil. Place on the hot grill, oiled side down. Cook—don't move them or they may stick—for 5 minutes for medium, brush the unoiled side with the rest of the oil, then turn and cook for another 5 minutes. (For well done, add an extra 1–2 minutes to each side.)

5 Remove and let the burgers rest for 2–3 minutes. Drizzle a little of the bell pepper juices over the bottom of each bun to moisten, lay on some watercress sprigs, and top with a burger, then a spoonful of the salsa, spooning over some more of the juices. Sandwich together with the tops of the buns.

OTHER WAYS TO USE ...

The meat mixture
Shape into meatballs and serve with spaghetti and a tomato sauce. Or omit the mustard and tarragon, replace with 1 tablespoon each chopped mint and oregano, and serve in pita bread with tomato, cucumber, and plain yogurt.

The salsa
Offer as an accompaniment to barbecued fish or chicken. Or serve as bruschetta, spooned onto slices of grilled, lightly oiled French bread.

Reduce fat by using lean ground beef and bulking the mixture out with shredded carrot

•

Brush oil on to the burgers directly, instead of the pan, to keep oil to a minimum

•

Flavor with mustard, garlic, and tarragon to reduce salt

•

Up veg and vitamin C by mixing carrots into the burger mix, using red bell peppers and tomatoes in the salsa, and replacing regular lettuce with watercress

Onion tart

This dish classically has a rich, buttery pastry, uses oil and butter for sautéing the onions, and a lot of cream and eggs to hold it all together. To turn things round, I tried a biscuitlike base that is lower in fat.

	Classic	Lighter
Kcals	604	309
Fat	49.7 g	16.6 g
Sat fat	26.8 g	7.4 g
Sodium	388 mg	336 mg

Per serving 309 kcals

Protein 9 g, carbs 33 g, fat 16.6 g, sat fat 7.4 g, fiber 2 g, sugar 8 g, sodium336 mg

Serves 6

Prep: 25 minutes
Cook: 45–50 minutes

For the filling

2 large red onions, halved lengthwise

2 tablespoons canola oil

2 large eggs

1 cup reduced-fat crème fraîche or light cream

1 teaspoon thyme leaves

1 teaspoon Dijon mustard

¼ cup shredded Gruyère cheese

For the crust

1⅓ cups all-purpose flour, plus extra for dusting

1¼ teaspoons baking powder

2 tablespoons cold butter, cut into small pieces

½ cup plain yogurt

¼ cup low-fat milk

salt and freshly ground black pepper

green salad, to serve

1 Slice the onions into small, thin, wedge-shape pieces. Heat the canola oil in a large, preferably nonstick sauté pan or deep skillet. Stir in the onions and sauté over medium heat for about 20 minutes. Stir only occasionally so that they can cook fairly undisturbed and caramelize underneath. When done, they should be well caramelized and sticky.

2 Meanwhile, prepare the crust. Preheat the oven to 375°F and put in a baking sheet. Put the flour, baking powder, and butter in a bowl with a pinch of salt and rub with your fingertips until it resembles rough crumbs. Mix the yogurt and milk together, pour into the flour mixture, and work together briefly with a knife until the dough just comes together. Remove from the bowl and gently press together to form a ball. Do not overwork.

3 Roll the dough out thinly on a lightly floured surface and use to line a 9 inch round, 1 inch deep, loose-bottom, fluted tart pan, pressing it with your fingers into the flutes. If the dough is a little sticky, dust your fingers in some of the flour.

4 Beat the eggs in a medium bowl, then stir in the crème fraîche, thyme, mustard, and seasoning. Spoon and spread half of the onions into the dough, season with black pepper, then sprinkle with half of the cheese. Pour the egg mixture over the top, then sprinkle with the rest of the onions and cheese. Sit the pan on the hot baking sheet and bake for 25–30 minutes, until the crust and filling are cooked. Remove and cool for about 10 minutes, then remove from the pan and serve while fresh and warm, with a green salad.

Instead of a rich flaky pastry, line a tart pan with a biscuit-type crust, which requires less fat

Chicken tikka masala

Like many Indian recipes, tikka masala needs to be done with a degree of authenticity using a core of key ingredients including cream and butter. This recipe tastes rich enough while massively cutting the fat content.

	Classic	Lighter
Kcals	566	515
Fat	40 g	10 g
Sat fat	13 g	2 g
Sodium	844 mg	120 mg

Per serving (with rice) 515 kcals

Protein 47 g, carbs 58 g, fat 10 g, sat fat 2 g, fiber 5 g, sugar 7 g, sodium 120 mg

Serves 4

Prep: 35 minutes, plus marinating and soaking
Cook: 35 minutes

For the marinade

2 inch piece fresh ginger root, peeled

4 plump garlic cloves, peeled

3 tablespoons plain yogurt

2 teaspoons lime juice

1 tablespoon finely chopped fresh cilantro leaves

½ teaspoon garam masala

½ teaspoon paprika

¼ teaspoon turmeric

¼–½ teaspoon hot chili powder

1 teaspoon cumin seeds

1 teaspoon coriander seeds

½ teaspoon fenugreek seeds

1¼ lb boneless, skinless chicken breasts, cut into 1½ inch chunks

For the sauce

2 tablespoons canola oil

2 onions, halved lengthwise and sliced into coarse, thin wedges

½ teaspoon paprika

½ teaspoon turmeric

½ teaspoon garam masala

¼ teaspoon hot chili powder (optional)

2 tablespoons tomato paste

2 tablespoons plain yogurt

For the rice

1⅓ cups basmati or long-grain rice

1⅓ cups frozen peas

salt

fresh cilantro leaves and lime wedges, to serve

1 For the marinade, finely grate the ginger and garlic (you should have 1 tablespoon of each), then mix them together. Put half of this mixture into a medium bowl, then stir in the yogurt, lime juice, chopped cilantro, garam masala, paprika, turmeric, and chili powder.

2 Heat a small, heavy, dry skillet, add the cumin, coriander, and fenugreek seeds, then heat briefly until toasted and smelling fragrant (they will start to jump in the pan). Remove and grind to a powder, using a mortar and pestle.

3 Stir half of the ground spices into the yogurt mixture (save the rest for the sauce). Stir the chicken chunks into the spiced yogurt until well coated. Cover and let marinate for at least 30 minutes or overnight in the refrigerator. Meanwhile, soak 8 wooden skewers in cold water for at least 30 minutes.

4 While the chicken is marinating, make the sauce. Heat the oil in a large saucepan. Add the onions, then sauté over medium heat for about 10 minutes, stirring occasionally, until softened and turning brown. Stir in the remaining ginger and garlic, then stir-fry for 2 minutes.

5 Mix the paprika, turmeric, garam masala, and chili powder, if using, into the onions with the rest of the toasted, ground spices. Cook for 1 minute, stirring to scrape up the sediment from the bottom of the pan. Stir in the tomato paste, then ⅔ cup water. Cook for 1 minute. Carefully transfer to a blender or food processor. Process to a thick, fairly smooth sauce. Return to the pan, pour in another ⅔ cup water, then set aside. The sauce can be made a day ahead. Soak the rice in cold water for up to 30 minutes.

6 Preheat the broiler to high. Thread the chicken onto the drained, soaked wooden skewers, then balance them across a baking pan lined with aluminum foil so that they are slightly raised over it. Broil for 12–15 minutes, turning often, until cooked through and slightly charred around the edges.

7 Meanwhile, drain the rice, then put it into a saucepan with 1½ cups of water. Bring to a boil, then cook over low heat, covered, for 8 minutes. Remove from the heat but keep covered for 5 minutes. Cook the peas in boiling water for 3 minutes, then drain. Fluff up the rice with a fork, then toss in the peas.

8 When ready to serve, reheat the sauce, stirring in any juices from the cooked chicken and a little more water to thin, if necessary (it should be thick). Remove from the heat, stir in the yogurt, then season with a pinch of salt. Serve the chicken skewers with the rice, a sprinkling of cilntro leaves, and lime wedges.

Eliminate cream and butter and use plain yogurt instead to reduce fat

•

Boost flavor by roasting some of the spices—and carefully balancing others—instead of adding salt

•

Use canola oil to lower saturated fat

Chicken cacciatore

An Italian classic that means "hunter's stew," this dish is often traditionally cooked with a whole, cut-up chicken, pancetta, and a good slug of olive oil. All delicious, but all help to increase the fat. With just a few small changes that don't affect the desired taste, fat and calories have been dramatically reduced.

	Classic	Lighter
Kcals	620	262
Fat	40.3 g	6.2 g
Sat fat	11.5 g	1.3 g
Sodium	640 mg	400 mg

Per serving 262 kcals

Protein 38.7 g, carbs 6.9 g, fat 6.2 g, sat fat 1.3 g, fiber 2.7 g, sugar 5.2 g, sodium 400 mg

Serves 4

Prep: 15 minutes
Cook: 50 minutes

1 tablespoon olive oil

3 slices prosciutto, trimmed of excess fat

1 medium onion, chopped

2 garlic cloves, finely chopped

2 sprigs of sage

2 sprigs of rosemary

4 (5 oz) boneless, skinless chicken breasts, preferably organic

⅔ cup dry white wine

1 (14½ oz) can plum tomatoes in natural juice

1 tablespoon tomato paste

8 oz cremini mushrooms, trimmed and quartered or halved if small

small handful of chopped flat leaf parsley

salt and freshly ground black pepper

1 Heat the oil in a large, nonstick skillet or sauté pan. Add the prosciutto and cook for about 2 minutes, until crisp. Remove with a slotted spoon, letting any fat drain back into the pan, and set aside. Put the onion, garlic, and sage and rosemary sprigs into the pan and sauté for 3–4 minutes, until the onion is starting to soften.

2 Spread the onion out in the bottom of the pan to make a bed of it, then lay the chicken breasts on top, skinned side down. Season with black pepper and cook for 5 minutes over medium heat, turning the chicken once, until starting to brown on both sides and the onion is caramelizing on the bottom of the pan. Raise the heat, give a quick stir, and, when all is sizzling, pour in the wine and let it simmer for 2 minutes to reduce slightly.

3 Lower the heat back to medium, return the prosciutto to the pan, then stir in the tomatoes (breaking them up with your spoon), tomato paste, and mushrooms. Pour 4–5 tablespoons water into the empty can of tomatoes, rinse it around, and pour it into the skillet. Cover and simmer for 30 minutes or until the chicken is cooked through, then cook, uncovered, for another 5 minutes so that the sauce can thicken slightly. Season with black pepper and a pinch of salt and serve sprinkled with the parsley.

choose lean, skinless chicken breasts and swap proscinto for fatty pancetta or bacon to reduce fat and saturated fat

LIGHT ENTERTAINING

Thai green chicken curry

Fresh and fragrant, real Thai curry has a carefully balanced mix of hot, sour, sweet and salty, with coconut milk an integral flavor. So this recipe focuses on how to achieve this using healthy ingredients and methods.

	Classic	Lighter
Kcals	817	487
Fat	44 g	16 g
Sat fat	32 g	10 g
Sodium	1,112 mg	384 mg

Per serving (with rice) 487 kcals

Protein 35 g, carbs 55 g, fat 16 g, sat fat 10 g, fiber 2 g, sugar 4 g, sodium 384 mg

Serves 4

Prep: 35 minutes
Cook: 20 minutes

For the curry paste

¼ bunch of fresh cilantro, stems and leaves separated

2 shallots, finely chopped

1 lemon grass stalk, finely chopped

2 garlic cloves, finely chopped

½ inch piece fresh ginger root, peeled and finely chopped

3 small hot green chiles, finely chopped (include the seeds)

1 larger, mild-to-medium green chile, finely chopped (include the seeds)

small handful of basil leaves

½ teaspoon ground cumin

½ teaspoon ground coriander

¼ teaspoon ground black pepper

1 teaspoon crumbled freeze-dried kaffir lime leaves

1 tablespoon lime juice

1 teaspoon sunflower oil

For the curry

1 tablespoon sunflower oil

1¾ cups reduced-fat coconut milk

3 (5 oz) boneless, skinless chicken breasts, cut into bite-size pieces

2 teaspoons Thai fish sauce

½ teaspoon granulated palm or light brown sugar

4 freeze-dried kaffir lime leaves

1½ cups snow peas, thinly sliced lengthwise

1 cup green beans, stem ends trimmed and halved lengthwise

finely shredded scallions and lime wedges, to serve

For the rice

1⅓ cups jasmine rice

1   For the curry paste, finely chop the cilantro stems and put them into a mini blender or small food processor with the shallots, lemon grass, garlic, and ginger. Pulse until it is as smooth as you can get it. Add the chiles, basil, three-quarters of the cilantro leaves, the ground cumin, coriander, black pepper, lime leaves, and lime juice, then pulse again. Mix in the oil and set aside. You will need only half of this paste; the rest can be chilled for a couple of days or frozen for up to a month.

2 For the curry, heat the oil in a nonstick wok or deep sauté pan, stir in half of the curry paste, then stir-fry for 1 minute. Stir the coconut milk until blended, then pour two-thirds into the pan. Let it simmer for 4–5 minutes, stirring now and then, until reduced and thickened slightly.

3 Cook the jasmine rice in a saucepan of boiling water, according to the package directions.

4 Meanwhile, add the chicken to the wok and stir-fry for 1–2 minutes, until no longer pink. Stir in the Thai fish sauce and sugar, then pour in the rest of the coconut milk to create a thinnish, creamy sauce. Lower the heat, add the lime leaves, then simmer for 5 minutes to gently finish cooking the chicken. The curry can be frozen at this point for up to 1 month.

5 While the chicken simmers, steam the snow peas and beans for a couple of minutes. Serve the curry in bowls with some of the vegetables piled on top (serve the rest separately) along with the scallions and the rest of the cilantro leaves. Accompany with a bowl of the cooked rice and lime wedges for squeezing over the curry.

Replace coconut cream with reduced-fat coconut milk, cooking it to thicken and enrich

•

Reduce the amount of oil to reduce the fat farther

•

Make your own curry paste to boost flavor and eliminate need for salt, as well as the need for using as much Thai fish sauce and sugar

Chicken balti

Recipes for this vary greatly. Spices can be different and all too often, excess fat is used, which makes it oily. This healthier version still has a kick and is a lot better for you than one prepared with ghee.

	Classic	Lighter
Kcals	309	217
Fat	15.4 g	6.6 g
Sat fat	6.1 g	1.3 g
Sodium	360 mg	200 mg

Per serving 217 kcals

protein 30.2 g, carbs 10.2 g, fat 6.6 g, sat fat 1.3 g, fiber 2.5 g, sugar 8.2 g, sodium 200 mg

Serves 4

Prep: 25 minutes plus marinating
Cook: 30 minutes

1 lb boneless, skinless chicken breasts, cut into bite-size pieces

1 tablespoon lime juice

1 teaspoon paprika

¼ teaspoon hot chili powder

1½ tablespoons sunflower oil or peanut oil

1 cinnamon stick

3 cardamom pods, lightly bashed to split

1 small to medium green chile

½ teaspoon cumin seeds

1 medium onion, coarsely grated

2 garlic cloves, minced

1 inch piece fresh root ginger, grated

½ teaspoon turmeric

1 teaspoon ground cumin

1 teaspoon ground coriander

1 teaspoon garam masala

1 cup tomato puree or tomato sauce

1 red bell pepper, cored, seeded, and cut into small chunks

1 medium tomato, chopped

3 cups baby spinach leaves

handful of fresh cilantro, chopped

salt and freshly ground black pepper

chapatis or basmati or other long-grain rice, to serve (optional)

1 Put the chicken in a nonmetallic medium bowl. Mix in the lime juice, paprika, chili powder, and a grinding of black pepper, then cover and let marinate for at least 15 minutes, preferably a little longer, in the refrigerator.

2 Heat 1 tablespoon of the oil in a large, nonstick wok or sauté pan. Add the cinnamon stick, cardamom pods, whole chile, and cumin seeds, and stir-fry briefly to just brown and release their fragrance. Stir in the onion, garlic, and ginger and sauté over medium-high heat for 3–4 minutes, until the onion starts to turn brown. Add the remaining oil, then drop in the chicken and stir-fry for 2–3 minutes or until it no longer looks raw. Mix together the turmeric, cumin, ground coriander, and garam masala. Add to the pan, lower the heat to medium, and cook for 2 minutes. Pour in the tomato puree and ⅔ cup water, then drop in the chunks of bell pepper. When starting to boil, lower the heat and simmer for 15–20 minutes or until the chicken is tender.

3 Stir in the tomato and simmer for 2–3 minutes, then add the spinach and turn it over in the pan to just wilt. Season with a little salt. If you want to thin down the sauce, splash in a little more water. Remove the cinnamon stick, chile, and cardamom pods, if you desire, before serving. Sprinkle with the fresh cilantro and serve with warm chapatis or basmati rice, if you desire.

cook in a nonstick wok to reduce the fat for cooking

•

stir in a lot of vegetables to increase your five a day

Salmon en croûte

Salmon wrapped in crisp, buttery pastry is one of those entertaining dishes that is valuable to have in your repertoire. This version uses phyllo pastry to reduce the fat by half, and loses none of the wow factor.

	Classic	Lighter
Kcals	634	331
Fat	44.9 g	20.2 g
Sat fat	17.2 g	4.1 g
Sodium	656 mg	188 mg

Per serving 331 kcals

Protein 26.6 g, carbs 11.6 g, fat 20.2 g, sat fat 4.1 g, fiber 1.1 g, sugar 1 g, sodium 188 mg

Serves 6

Prep: 30 minutes, plus cooling
Cook: 35 minutes

3 tablespoons olive oil

2 large shallots, finely chopped

5 oz cremini mushrooms, trimmed and finely chopped

3 garlic cloves, finely chopped

juice of ½ lemon

4 oz watercress, chopped

2 tablespoons snipped dill

1 tablespoon snipped chives

2½ tablespoons reduced-fat crème fraîche or light cream

6 sheets phyllo pastry, each about 15 x 12 inches

2 (12 oz) skinned salmon fillets

salt and freshly ground black pepper

1 Heat 2 tablespoons of the oil in a large, nonstick skillet. Sauté the shallots for 2–3 minutes to soften, then add the mushrooms and garlic and stir-fry over high heat for another 3–4 minutes or until the mushrooms and shallots are golden and any liquid from the mushrooms has evaporated. Pour in the lemon juice; after a few seconds, that should evaporate, too. Remove from the heat, then stir in the watercress until it wilts. Stir in the dill and chives, and season with a little salt and black pepper. Let cool.

2 Preheat the oven to 400°F. Line a baking sheet with parchment paper. When the mushroom mixture is cool, stir in the crème fraîche. Lay one of the phyllo sheets on the work surface with a short end facing you. Brush all over with a little of the remaining oil. Layer up 4 more of the phyllo sheets in the same way, brushing each with a little of the oil.

3 Lay one of the salmon fillets, skin side up, across the width of the phyllo, positioning it about one-third of the way up. Season it with black pepper. Spoon and spread the cooled mushroom mixture over the top of the fish. Lay the other salmon fillet on top, skin side down. Season again. Fold the short end of pastry nearest to you over the salmon, then bring the other end over to completely enclose the salmon, lifting it so that the you can tuck the seam under it. Fold both pastry ends over as neatly as you can.

4 Brush the outside with a little more of the remaining oil. Scrunch up the last sheet of phyllo, pressing it lightly on top in big folds, then carefully brush with the last of the oil. The dish can be prepared 3–4 hours ahead up to this point and chilled.

5 Transfer the salmon package to the baking sheet. Bake for 25 minutes, until the pastry is crisp and golden brown. Check while it cooks, and if the top starts to brown too quickly, lay a sheet of aluminum foil loosely over it. Remove from the oven and let the salmon sit for 2–3 minutes before slicing.

use a nonstick skillet so that you can use less oil

•

Replace puff pastry with phyllo to greatly reduce both fat and calories

•

Include mushrooms to increase the levels of the B vitamins, and watercress, also for its B vitamins as well as iron and minerals

•

use reduced-fat crème fraîche instead of heavy cream to reduce fat farther

•

Glaze pastry with oil instead of egg

Spaghetti carbonara

It's one of the most popular pasta dishes, but with heavy cream, cheese, eggs, and salty, fatty bacon in the original, this lighter version is sure to become a new favorite.

	Classic	Lighter
Kcals	935	527
Fat	49.8 g	16.1 g
Sat fat	21.9 g	6.3 g
Sodium	1,492 mg	652 mg

Per serving 527 kcals

Protein 29.7 g, carbs 70 g, fat 16.1 g, sat fat 6.3 g, fiber 5.2 g, sugar 4.4 g, sodium 652 mg

Serves 4

Prep: 15 minutes
Cook: 20 minutes

2 extra-large eggs

1⅓ cups frozen peas

12 oz spaghetti

1 tablespoon olive oil

4 oz lean back bacon, trimmed of excess fat, chopped into small pieces

2 plump garlic cloves, finely chopped

1 cup grated Parmesan cheese

salt and freshly ground black pepper

handful of snipped chives, to garnish

1 Bring a large saucepan of water to a boil with a pinch of salt. Beat the eggs in a bowl with a little black pepper. Cook the peas in a boiling water for 2–3 minutes, drain, reserving the water, and set aside.

2 Return the pea cooking water to the pan, bring back to a boil, and cook the spaghetti until al dente, following the package directions. While the spaghetti is cooking, heat the oil in a large, deep skillet or sauté pan. Cook the bacon for several minutes, until it starts to turn crisp. Stir in the garlic and cook briefly until pale brown. Add the peas, and if the spaghetti isn't quite ready, keep it warm over low heat.

3 When the pasta is done, remove the pan with the bacon from the heat. Lift the spaghetti out of its pan with a pair of tongs (reserving the cooking water) and drop it into the skillet with the garlic, bacon, and peas. Mix most of the cheese into the eggs, reserving a handful of cheese for sprinkling over each serving. Quickly pour in the eggs and cheese, lifting and stirring with the tongs so that everything mixes well and the spaghetti is coated. Ladle in a little of the reserved pasta water, enough to coat the spaghetti and create some sauce in the pan.

4 Spoon or twirl the pasta into shallow serving bowls using a long pronged fork. Serve immediately with a sprinkling of the reserved cheese, some snipped chives, and a grinding of black pepper.

Eliminate cream and use the pasta water to create a sauciness

Nasi goreng

This is Indonesia's equivalent to China's popular fried rice, but when generous amounts of soy sauce are splashed in, it can quickly become high in sodium. This recipe shows there are plenty of other ways to enhance flavor, trim the fat, and still keep its unique taste.

	Classic	Lighter
Kcals	694	405
Fat	27.2 g	7.9 g
Sat fat	4.6 g	1.2 g
Sodium	1,160 mg	640 mg

Per serving 405 kcals

Protein 30.7 g, carbs 50.9 g, fat 7.9g, sat fat 1.2 g, fiber 4.6 g, sugar 3.6 g, sodium 640 mg

Serves 4

Prep: 30 minutes
Cook: 20 minutes

1¼ cups trimmed and quartered widthwise green beans

1 extra-large egg

1 tablespoon low-fat milk

generous pinch of turmeric

2 tablespoons canola oil

1¼ cups white long-grain rice

½ cup fresh or frozen peas

3 shallots, finely chopped

2 garlic cloves, finely chopped

1 red Thai chile, seeded and finely chopped (or keep a few seeds in for extra heat)

2 (5 oz) boneless, skinless, chicken breasts, cut into 1 inch cubes

1 teaspoon paprika

1 teaspoon ground coriander

4 oz cooked, peeled shrimp

To serve

3 scallions, ends trimmed

4 teaspoons dark soy sauce

½ cup diced cucumber

handful of chopped fresh cilantro

lime wedges

salt and freshy ground black pepper

1 Steam (or boil) the beans for 4–5 minutes, until tender-crisp. Drain if necessary, then run them under running cold water to stop them from cooking farther. Set aside.

2 Make an omelet. Beat the egg in a bowl, then mix in the milk and turmeric and some black pepper. Pour 1 teaspoon of the oil into a large, nonstick skillet. Pour in the egg and swirl the pan around so that the bottom is completely covered to make a thin omelet about 9 inches in diameter. Cook over medium heat for 1–2 minutes (there is no need to turn it over) until set on top and lightly browned underneath. Slide the omelet onto a board with the browned side underneath, roll it up tightly like a log, then cut across into thin slices. Set aside.

3 If you want to curl the scallions for a garnish, halve each one, then slice into long, thin shreds. Put in a small bowl, cover with cold water, and let sit in the refrigerator to curl.

4 Cook the rice in a saucepan of boiling water for about 10 minutes or until just tender, adding the peas for the last 3 minutes.

5 While the rice is cooking, heat 1 tablespoon of the oil in a large sauté pan or wok, add the shallots, garlic, and chile, and stir-fry for 2–3 minutes, until softening and tinged brown. Pour in another 1 teaspoon of the oil, stir in the chicken, and stir-fry for 4–5 minutes, until cooked. Stir in the paprika, ground coriander, shrimp, and beans and cook for another 1 minute to heat everything through and cook the spices.

6 Drain the rice in a colander, and if you are still cooking the chicken, sit the colander over a saucepan with a little gently boiling water in the bottom and cover the rice with the lid so that it can dry off slightly and keep warm in the steam.

7 Mix the cooked rice and sliced omelet into the chicken and gently stir to reheat well. Season with bell pepper and just a little salt. Serve each portion drizzled with a little of the rest of the oil and 1 teaspoon of the soy sauce, then sprinkle with some cucumber and chopped cilantro and top with a small pile of the drained, shredded scallions.

TIP

- Traditionally, this dish is made as a way of using up leftover cooked rice. Here, it is cooked fresh to make it an instant meal, but if you do use leftover rice, it is important to cool it quickly after initial cooking, keep it in the refrigerator until ready to use, then reheat thoroughly before serving.

Lower fat and saturated fat by using lean, skinless chicken breast

•

Reduce fat farther by cooking in a nonstick skillet and using less egg but extending it with low-fat milk

•

Lower sodium by using fewer shrimp and less soy sauce. Keep flavor up with extra spices and drizzle dark soy sauce over at the end for a direct taste hit

•

Include green beans and peas to improve your five a day and fiber content

Coq au vin

A rich and satisfying dish, ideal for winter entertaining. Best of all, this lighter version comes with the same deep flavor, but the fat and calories are greatly reduced. Keep the whole meal lighter and serve with Braised leeks and peas (see p. 202) and Creamy Mashed Potatoes (see p. 213).

	Classic	Lighter
Kcals	818	420
Fat	53.8 g	13.2 g
Sat fat	18.1 g	3.2 g
Sodium	480 mg	560 mg

Per serving 420 kcals

Protein 46.9 g, carbs 7.3 g, fat 13.2 g, sat fat 3.2 g, fiber 1.3 g, sugar 1.7 g, sodium 560 mg

Serves 6

Prep: 25 minutes
Cook: 1 hour 15–35 minutes

3 sprigs of thyme

2 sprigs of rosemary

2 bay leaves

3 tablespoons olive oil

4 oz dry-cured smoked bacon, trimmed of excess fat, chopped

12 small shallots, peeled

2 (8 oz) chicken legs, skin removed

4 (6 oz) chicken thighs with bone and skin, skin removed

2 (5 oz) boneless, skinless chicken breasts

3 garlic cloves, finely chopped

3 tablespoons brandy

2½ cups red wine

⅔ cup good-quality chicken stock

2 teaspoons tomato paste

9 oz cremini mushrooms, trimmed and halved if large

For the thickening paste

2 tablespoons all-purpose flour

1½ teaspoons olive oil

1 teaspoon butter, softened

salt and freshly ground black pepper

small handful of chopped flat leaf parsley, to garnish

1 Tie the herbs together with kitchen string or in a cheesecloth bag to make a bouquet garni.

2 Heat 1 tablespoon of the oil in a large, heavy saucepan, dutch oven, or flameproof casserole. Add the bacon and cook until crisp. Remove and drain on paper towels. Add the shallots to the pan and sauté, stirring or shaking the pan often, for 5–8 minutes, until well browned all over. Remove and set aside with the bacon.

3 Pat the chicken pieces dry with paper towels. Pour ½ tablespoon of the remaining oil into the pan, then cook half the chicken pieces, turning regularly, for 5–8 minutes, until well browned. Remove, then repeat with the remaining chicken. Remove and set aside.

4 Add the garlic and sauté briefly, then, with the heat medium-high, pour in the brandy, stirring the bottom of the pan to deglaze. The alcohol should sizzle and start to evaporate so there is not much left.

5 Return the chicken legs and thighs to the pan along with any juices, then pour in a little of the wine, stirring the bottom of the pan again. Stir in the rest of the wine, the stock, and tomato paste, drop in the bouquet garni, season with black pepper and a pinch of salt, then return the bacon and shallots to the pan. Cover, lower the heat to a gentle simmer, add the chicken breasts, and cook for 50 minutes–1 hour.

6 Just before serving, heat the remaining oil in a large, nonstick skillet. Add the mushrooms and sauté over high heat for a few minutes, until golden. Remove and keep warm.

7 Lift the chicken, shallots, and bacon from the pan and transfer to a warm serving dish. Remove the bouquet garni.

8 For the thickening paste, mix the flour, olive oil, and butter in a small bowl using the back of a teaspoon. Bring the wine mixture to a gentle boil, then gradually drop in small pieces of the thickening paste, whisking each piece in with a wire whisk. Simmer for 1–2 minutes.

9 Sprinkle the mushrooms over the chicken, then pour the wine sauce over the poultry. Garnish with the chopped parsley.

Remove skin from the chicken to reduce fat

•

Replace some of the butter with oil to lower saturated fat

•

Boost flavor with herbs so that less salt is needed

Lamb tagine

With the exotic combination of meat, spices, fruits, and nuts in a Moroccan tagine, or stew, fat can easily tip the balance from low to high, depending on how it is cooked and the choice of meat. By choosing a lean cut of lamb and considering other ways to lighten, this recipe has more than halved the fat without losing any of its appeal.

	Classic	Lighter
Kcals	534	339
Fat	33.4 g	14.7 g
Sat fat	13.3 g	4.4 g
Sodium	280 mg	240 mg

Per serving 339 kcals

Protein 29.9 g, carbs 22.5 g, fat 14.7 g, sat fat 4.4 g, fiber 6 g, sugar 15.3 g, sodium 240 mg

Serves 6

Prep: 35 minutes, plus overnight marinating
Cook: 2 hours 25 minutes

1½ lb diced leg of lamb, cut into about 1½ inch pieces, trimmed of excess fat

2 medium onions

2 teaspoons ground cumin

1½ teaspoons paprika

1 teaspoon ground cinnamon

good pinch of crushed red pepper flakes

good pinch of saffron threads

2 tablespoons canola oil

3 garlic cloves, finely chopped

1½ teaspoons finely grated fresh ginger root

1½ (14½ oz) cans plum tomatoes

1 cup bunch fresh cilantro

1 cup halved dried apricots

1 (15 oz) can chickpeas, drained

2 teaspoons honey

salt and freshly ground black pepper

1 Preheat the oven to 325°F. Put the meat in a large mixing bowl. Grate one of the onions, then add it to the meat with the cumin, paprika, cinnamon, red pepper flakes, saffron, and 1 tablespoon of the oil. Season well with black pepper and toss well together to coat. Cover and let stand for 2–3 hours or preferably overnight in the refrigerator.

2 Chop the remaining onion. Heat the remaining oil in a large, heavy nonstick skillet or sauté pan. Put in the chopped onion, garlic, and ginger and cook over medium heat for about 5 minutes, stirring often, until starting to brown. Then raise the heat slightly, add the meat and its spices, and stir-fry until it's no longer pink. Stir in the canned tomatoes. Rinse the cans out with 1 cup water and stir in. Chop half of the bunch of cilantro, including the stems, and stir it into the stew with the apricots. Heat through and transfer to an ovenproof dish.

3 Cook in the oven for 2 hours, topping up with a little more water, if necessary to keep it all juicy. Stir in the chickpeas and honey and cook for another 15 minutes or until the meat is really tender.

4 Separate the leaves from the remaining cilantro and chop. Season the stew with a little salt and serve sprinkled with the chopped cilantro leaves.

Replace some of the meat with chickpeas to keep the protein up but reduce the fat, boost fiber content, and count toward your five a day

Salmon teriyaki

It's a popular restaurant dish, but sodium and sugar can be high in this Japanese speciality, due to the sticky, salty-sweetness of the sauce. By adjusting some of the traditional ingredients and combining with handy pantry ones, it's quick to make at home, and sodium is halved and sugar greatly lowered, but the familiar taste remains.

	Classic	Lighter
Kcals	361	269
Fat	18.2 g	15.4 g
Sat fat	3 g	2.7 g
Sugar	11.3 g	1.6 g
Sodium	1,160 mg	600 mg

Per serving 269 kcals

Protein 28.7 g, carbs 2 g, fat 15.4 g, sat fat 2.7 g, fiber 0.1 g, sugar 1.6 g, sodium 600 mg

Serves 4

Prep: 10 minutes
Cook: 15 minutes

2 tablespoons dark soy sauce

3 tablespoons dry white wine

2 tablespoons apple juice from concentrate

2 teaspoons white wine vinegar

2 garlic cloves, crushed

1 teaspoon finely grated fresh ginger root

4 (5 oz) salmon fillets, skinned

freshly ground black pepper

1 Make the teriyaki sauce. Put the soy sauce, wine, apple juice, vinegar, garlic, and ginger in a small saucepan with 1 tablespoon water and a grinding of black pepper. Bring to a boil, then simmer for 2–3 minutes to reduce slightly. Remove and set aside.

2 Heat the broiler to high. Line a baking sheet with aluminum foil and lay the salmon fillets on it. Broil the salmon, fairly near the heat source, for about 10 minutes or until done (no need to turn it), brushing a couple of times with a little of the teriyaki sauce for the last 2 minutes to glaze.

3 Warm the rest of the sauce and pour it over the salmon to serve.

TIPS

• To check when the salmon is cooked, open up the flesh slightly in the middle with the tip of a sharp knife, and if you like it cooked all the way through, the flakes should no longer look translucent.

• Serve with fine noodles tossed with chopped fresh cilantro—and a fresh green vegetable.

Extend the sauce with apple juice, which provides natural sweetness, instead of adding sugar

Mediterranean fish stew

Packed with fish, seafood, and tomatoes, this dish is a pretty healthy classic. To improve things even more, it's only taken a few tweaks to maximize its benefits and lower sodium and fat.

	Classic	Lighter
Kcals	311	255
Fat	7.5 g	5.2 g
Sat fat	1.1 g	0.8 g
Sodium	720 mg	360 mg

Per serving 255 kcals

Protein 30.8 g, carbs 12.9 g, fat 5.2 g, sat fat 0.8 g, fiber 6 g, sugar 9 g, sodium 360 mg

Serves 4

Prep: 20 minutes
Cook: 25 minutes

1 fennel bulb

1 tablespoon olive oil, plus 1 teaspoon

1 small carrot, diced

2 celery sticks, diced

1 large or 2 small shallots, finely chopped

2 garlic cloves, finely chopped

¾ cup dry white wine

⅓ cup tomato juice

1 (14½ oz) can cherry tomatoes, in natural juice

good pinch of saffron threads

good pinch of smoked paprika

¼ cup chopped basil

16 cherry tomatoes on the vine

1 lb 2oz skinless haddock, halibut, or cod fillets, cut into 1½–2 inch chunks

12 raw (or cooked), peeled jumbo shrimp, with tails left on

salt and freshly ground pepper

include fennel, carrot, and celery and extra cherry tomatoes to top up the five a day, vitamin C, fiber, and flavor

1 Preheat the oven to 400°F. Trim, then quarter the fennel lengthwise and cut out and discard the central core. Finely chop the fennel. Heat the 1 tablespoon oil in a large, deep sauté pan or skillet. Add the fennel, carrot, celery, shallot, and garlic and sauté for 3–4 minutes. Increase the heat, pour in the wine, and simmer for a few minutes, until reduced by one-third. Mix the tomato juice with ⅔ cup of water. Pour into the pan with the can of tomatoes, saffron, paprika, and 2 tablespoons of the basil. Season with black pepper, bring to a boil, then simmer gently for about 8 minutes to cook the vegetables and reduce the liquid slightly.

2 While the vegetables are cooking, remove the tomatoes from the vine and cut in half widthwise. Lay them on a baking sheet, sprinkle with 1 tablespoon of the remaining basil, season with black pepper, and drizzle with the 1 teaspoon oil. Roast in the oven for 8–10 minutes, until the tomatoes are softened but still holding their shape.

3 Place the fish and shrimp (if using raw ones) in the sauté pan with the vegetables and simmer gently for 4–5 minutes or until they are just cooked and no longer opaque. If using cooked shrimp, add them for the last minute or two to heat through. Season with a pinch of salt.

4 Spoon the fish and vegetables into the middle of large, wide bowls, spoon the liquid around them, and serve topped with the roasted tomatoes and sprinkled with the last of the chopped basil.

Risotto primavera

This dish is mainly rice cooked with a lot of fresh green seasonal vegetables, but there are hidden extras. Butter is often used to sauté the rice at the beginning, and a generous amount is usually stirred in at the end—as is Parmesan—to inject flavor and richness. I looked at what could be added instead to develop the flavor.

	Classic	Lighter
Kcals	715	475
Fat	31 g	10.4 g
Sat fat	16 g	2.8 g
Sodium	840 mg	120 mg

Per serving 475 kcals

Protein 18.6 g, carbs 70.5 g, fat 10.4 g, sat fat 2.8 g, fiber 9.8 g, sugar 5.2 g, sodium 120 mg

Serves 4

Prep: 40 minutes
Cook: 35 minutes

2 tablespoons olive oil

12 oz asparagus spears, trimmed and sliced into 2 inch diagonal lengths

9 scallions, ends trimmed and sliced

1 cup fresh or frozen peas

1⅔ cups shelled fresh or frozen fava beans

2 tablespoons shredded basil

2 tablespoons snipped chives

1 tablespoon finely chopped mint

finely grated zest of 1 lemon

7 cups vegetable stock

4 shallots, finely chopped

3 plump garlic cloves, finely chopped

1½ cups risotto rice

⅔ cup dry white wine

¼ cup grated Parmesan cheese or vegetarian alternative

1 cup arugula

freshly ground black pepper

1 Heat half the oil in a large, wide nonstick skillet. Add the asparagus and stir-fry over medium-high heat for about 4 minutes or until nicely browned all over. Stir in the scallions and sauté for 1–2 minutes with the asparagus until browned. Remove, season with black pepper, and set aside.

2 Cook the peas and beans separately in a little boiling water for 3 minutes each, then drain each through a strainer. When the fava beans are cool enough to handle, pop them out of their skins. Set the peas and beans aside.

3 Mix together the basil, chives, mint, and lemon zest in a small bowl and season with black pepper. Set aside.

4 Pour the stock into a saucepan and keep it on low heat. Pour the remaining oil into a large, wide sauté pan. Add the shallots and garlic and sauté for 3–4 minutes, until soft and only slightly brown. Stir in the rice and continue to stir for 1–2 minutes over medium-high heat. As it starts to sizzle, pour in

the wine and stir again until the wine has been absorbed. Start to stir in the hot stock, 1½ ladlefuls at a time, so that it simmers and is absorbed after each addition. Keep stirring the whole time to keep the risotto creamy. Continue adding the stock as above; after 20 minutes the rice should be soft with a bit of chew in the middle. If it isn't, add more stock; you should still have at least a ladleful of stock left at this point. Season with black pepper; you shouldn't need to add any salt.

5 Remove the pan from the heat. Pour over a ladleful of the remaining stock to keep the mixture fluid, then spread all the vegetables over top along with a grinding of black pepper, half of the herb mixture, and half of the cheese. Cover and let the risotto sit for 3–4 minutes to rest. Gently stir everything together, adding a drop more remaining stock for good consistency, if necessary. Ladle into serving dishes and serve topped with a small pile of arugula and the remaining herbs and cheese sprinkled over the top.

OTHER WAYS TO USE …

The cooked rice mixture
Instead of stirring spring vegetables through at the end, sprinkle the rice with a mix of roasted vegetables, such as bell peppers, zucchini, onion, and squash. Or instead of a main meal, serve the finished risotto as an accompaniment to broiled chicken or poached salmon.

Replace butter with olive oil, using less of it

•

Increase the vegetables to provide three of your five-a-day

•

Reduce the amount of Parmesan to lower the fat farther

•

Mix in a lemon zest and herb mixture for extra flavor instead of extra salt

Beef Wellington

In classic recipes for this impressive entertaining centerpiece, there is layer upon layer of rich ingredients. For my healthier version, I wanted to maintain the extravagant look and taste while greatly reducing the calories and fat. The meat needs to be tied at equal intervals to hold it together—either do this yourself or ask your butcher to do it.

	Classic	Lighter
Kcals	699	350
Fat	41 g	16.6 g
Sat fat	19.3 g	5 g
Sodium	680 mg	320 mg

Per serving 350 kcals

Protein 39.5 g, carbs 8.3 g, fat 16.6 g, sat fat 5 g, fiber 1.3 g, sugar 0.8 g, sodium 320 mg

Serves 6

Prep: 1 hour, plus soaking, cooling, and resting
Cook: about 1 hour

For the beef

3 tablespoons canola oil

2¼ lb thick, lean beef tenderloin, tied at equal intervals

good handful of dried porcini

2 shallots, finely chopped

2 garlic cloves, finely chopped

5 oz cremini mushrooms, trimmed and finely chopped

2 tablespoons finely chopped flat leaf parsley

1 tablespoon finely chopped tarragon

4 cups mix of watercress, baby spinach, and arugula or watercress or spinach leaves or other peppery salad green mixture

6 sheets phyllo pastry, each about 15 x 12 inches

For the gravy

1 teaspoon all-purpose flour

⅓ cup red wine

1½ cups chicken stock

2 teaspoons Dijon mustard

salt and freshly ground black pepper

1 Preheat the oven to 425°F. Heat 2 teaspoons of the oil in a large, nonstick skillet. Lay the beef in the pan and cook over high heat for 5 minutes to seal, turning often. Transfer it to a roasting pan, season with black pepper and a pinch of salt, then roast for 17–18 minutes (this roasts to medium-rare).

2 Meanwhile, put the porcini in a small heatproof bowl, cover with boiling water, and let stand for 20–30 minutes to soak.

3 Pour 1 tablespoon of the remaining oil into the same skillet (don't wash it) that the meat was cooked in. Add the shallots, garlic, and cremini mushrooms and sauté for 4–5 minutes, stirring often, over high heat so that all the liquid is first released from the mushrooms, then evaporated, and all are softened. Remove from the heat, stir in the parsley and tarragon, season with black pepper and a pinch of salt, and let cool.

4 Put the mixture of leaves in a large heatproof bowl, pour over boiling water, let stand for 30 seconds, then transfer to a colander, rinse under cold running water, and drain. Squeeze out all the moisture with your hands and pat dry with paper towels. Chop and set aside.

5 Drain the porcini, reserving ⅓ cup of the soaking liquid for the gravy. Chop the porcini finely and stir it into the mushroom mixture. Line a baking sheet with parchment paper.

6 When the beef is done, remove from the oven and let it sit in the pan for 10 minutes for any juices to be released. Lower the oven temperature to 400°F. Lift the beef from the pan (keep all the juices in the pan for the gravy) and lay it on paper towels. Let sit until dry and cool enough to wrap in the phyllo pastry.

7 Lay one of the phyllo sheets on the work surface with a short end facing you. Brush all over with a little of the remaining oil. Layer up and oil 4 more phyllo sheets in the same way. Remove the string from the cooled beef. Spread the chopped leaves down the middle of the pastry so that it is the same length and width as the beef. Top with the mushroom mixture and lightly press down. Lay the beef over this, with the top of the beef facing down. Bring the long sides of the phyllo over the beef to enclose it, then turn it over so that the seam is underneath. Tuck both ends of the pastry under (trim first, if necessary, to reduce any excess) and place on the lined baking sheet so that all the seams are on the bottom. Brush with more oil.

8 Lay the last sheet of phyllo on the work surface in front of you, with one of the longest sides toward you, then cut across its width into 5 strips. Lay these one by one, slightly overlapping, over the wrapped beef, scrunching up an edge of each strip slightly as you work to create some height. Carefully brush with the last of the oil, then bake for 30 minutes, until golden. If the pastry starts to brown too quickly, loosely lay a piece of aluminum foil over the top. Remove the meat and let sit for 5–10 minutes before slicing.

9 Meanwhile, make the gravy. Heat the saved roasting juices in the roasting pan, stirring to deglaze. Stir in the flour. Gradually pour in the wine, stirring all the time to blend in the flour. Stir in the stock and reserved porcini liquid and simmer for 8–10 minutes to reduce a little. It should have body, but be thinner like a "jus." Stir in the mustard and season with black pepper. Transfer the beef to a plate, then slice thickly with a sharp knife and serve with a spoonful or two of the gravy.

OTHER WAYS TO USE ...

The filling

The wilted leaves and mushroom mixture make a great topping for chicken, salmon, or other fish fillets. Lay both the leaves and mushroom mixture on top of skinned chicken breasts or fish fillets, wrap in parchment paper packages, then bake.

Replace puff pastry with phyllo to greatly reduce the fat

•

Eliminate butter and use canola oil instead to keep saturated fat levels down

•

Use a nonstick skillet

•

Make a light mushroom mixture instead of classic pâté

•

Use herbs, garlic, and porcini to give flavor so that less salt is needed

Eggplant Parmigiana

I've always thought this recipe needed generous amounts of oil to make it as delicious as it is. But by working out a lighter way to cook the eggplants, I've discovered that it's not really necessary. So combined with swapping cheeses, this dish hasn't lost its richness, but has reduced the fat by more than half.

	Classic	Lighter
Kcals	394	213
Fat	31.3 g	14.4 g
Sat fat	13.2 g	5.7 g
Sodium	880 mg	240 mg

Per serving 213 kcals

Protein 10.8 g, carbs 10.2 g, fat 14.4 g, sat fat 5.7 g, fiber 6.9 g, sugar 9.4 g, sodium 240 mg

Serves 4

Prep: 35 minutes
Cook: 40 minutes

2 tablespoons olive oil, plus 1 teaspoon

1½ tablespoons lemon juice

3 small eggplants

2 garlic cloves, finely chopped

1½ (14½ oz) cans plum tomatoes

1 tablespoon tomato paste

1 tablespoon chopped basil, plus handful of leaves and extra leaves to garnish

½ cup ricotta cheese

2 oz mozzarella cheese

2 medium tomatoes, sliced

¼ cup grated Parmesan cheese

salt and freshly ground black pepper

1 Preheat the oven to 400°F. Brush a little of the 2 tablespoons oil onto 2–3 large, nonstick baking sheets (or 1 sheet if baking the eggplants in batches). Mix the rest of the 2 tablespoons oil with the lemon juice. Slice the eggplants into ½ inch-thick slices lengthwise and lay them in a single layer on the oiled baking sheets. Brush with the oil and lemon mixture, then season with black pepper. Bake for about 25 minutes, until golden and softened, turning halfway through if necessary.

2 Meanwhile, make a tomato sauce. Heat the 1 teaspoon oil in a medium saucepan. Add the garlic and sauté for 1 minute. Stir in the canned tomatoes, breaking them down with a wooden spoon as you stir. Mix in the tomato paste and the 1 tablespoon chopped basil. Season with black pepper and a pinch of salt, then simmer for about 15 minutes to thicken slightly and make a spoonable sauce.

3 Spread a spoonful or two of the sauce (just a thin layer) in the bottom of a shallow ovenproof dish, about 10 x 8 x 2 inches. Layer one-third of the baked eggplants on top, in overlapping slices. Spread over one-third of the remaining sauce and dot half of the ricotta in small spoonfuls on the sauce. Half of the mozzarella, tear, and sprinkle it over the eggplants with half of the basil leaves, then season with black pepper. Repeat this layering with the eggplants, sauce, ricotta, mozzarella, and basil, finishing with the last third of the eggplants followed by the last of the sauce. Lay the sliced tomatoes over the sauce, season with black pepper, then sprinkle with the Parmesan.

4 Bake at the same oven temperature as before for about 15 minutes or until golden and bubbling. Serve sprinkled with extra basil leaves.

Lower the calories and the fat farther by replacing most of the mozzarella with ricotta cheese

Fish casserole

This fish casserole is much easier to make than a traditional British fish "pie"—there's no fussy about with a roux sauce or mashing potatoes for the classic mash-potato topping. My tasters loved the rich combination of creamy sauce, chunky fish, and crisp topping despite the fact that I'd managed to lower the saturated fat by more than three-quarters.

	Classic	Lighter
Kcals	676	413
Fat	38 g	15 g
Sat fat	19 g	4 g
Sodium	488 mg	568 mg

Per serving 413 kcals

Protein 42 g, carbs 30 g, fat 15 g, sat fat 4 g, fiber 2 g, sugar 7 g, sodium 568 mg

Serves 6

Prep: 30 minutes, plus cooling
Cook: about 1 hour

2 cups low-fat milk

3 tablespoons cornstarch

4 oz cooked shrimp in their shells

several sprigs of thyme, preferably lemon thyme

2 bay leaves

1 garlic clove, thinly sliced

1¾ lb unpeeled new potatoes, scrubbed

1 medium leek, trimmed, cleaned, and thinly sliced

14 oz skinless haddock, halibut, or red snapper fillet

12 oz skinless salmon fillet

6 oz skinless smoked haddock fillet

½ cup low-fat cream cheese with garlic and herbs

2 tablespoons finely chopped parsley

2 tablespoons olive oil

2 tablespoons snipped chives

freshly ground black pepper

1 Mix 3 tablespoons of the milk into the cornstarch and set aside. Pour the rest of the milk into a saucepan. Peel the shrimp, reserve the meat, then drop the shells and heads (wash them first, if necessary) into the milk along with the sprigs of thyme, bay leaves, garlic, and a grind of black pepper. Bring to a boil, then remove from the heat and let steep for 20 minutes.

2 Meanwhile, put the potatoes into a large saucepan of water, bring to a boil, and simmer for 20 minutes, until tender. Drain.

3 Steam the sliced leek for 3 minutes, then remove from the heat and set aside.

4 Strain the steeped milk through a strainer into a large, shallow sauté pan. Lay the fish fillets in the milk. Bring to a boil, then lower the heat and simmer gently for 3 minutes. Remove from the heat and let stand, covered, for 5 minutes. Use a slotted spoon to transfer all the fish to a dish and let cool slightly. Preheat the oven to 400°F.

5 Stir the slackened cornstarch, then stir it into the hot milk in the sauté pan. Return the pan to the heat and stir until thickened. Briefly stir in the cream cheese, remove from the heat, then add the parsley and season with black pepper. Stir in any liquid that has drained from the fish. Break the fish into big pieces and place them in a 2 quart ovenproof dish. Spread with the shrimp and leek, then season with black pepper. Pour the sauce over the top and give a few gentle stirs to evenly distribute the sauce and combine everything without breaking up the fish.

6 Using a large fork, crush the potatoes by breaking them up (not mashing them) into chunky pieces. Mix in the oil, chives, and a grind of black pepper. Spoon the crushed potatos over the fish. Place the dish on a baking sheet and bake for 25–30 minutes or until the sauce is bubbling and the potatoes golden brown. Alternatively, make the dish completely, refrigerate it for several hours or overnight, then bake at the same temperature as above for 45 minutes.

OTHER WAYS TO USE ...

The fish and leek sauce
Gently mix it all together and serve over shell-shape pasta.

cut butter and cream from the sauce and add creaminess with light cream cheese. intensify the taste by steeping the milk with flavorings

•

instead of a buttery, cheesy mashed potatoes, try crushed potatos using olive oil

Chicken biryani

My challenge was to reduce the fat and sodium, yet still retain the intricacies of the recipe with its gentle, fragrant spicing and rich, moist consistency. Serve with a cooling tomato and cucumber raita.

	Classic	Lighter
Kcals	674	485
Fat	30.5 g	11.7 g
Sat fat	6.5 g	1.5 g
Sodium	800 mg	240 mg

Per serving 485 kcals

Protein 40.1 g, carbs 51.7 g, fat 11.7 g, sat fat 1.5 g, fiber 2.7 g, sugar 7.1 g, sodium 240 mg

Serves 5

Prep: 25 minutes, plus marinating and steeping
Cook: 1¼ hours

3 garlic cloves, finely grated

2 teaspoons finely grated fresh ginger root

¼ teaspoon ground cinnamon

1 teaspoon turmeric

⅓ cup plain yogurt

1¼ lb boneless, skinless chicken breasts, cut into 2 inch pieces

2 tablespoons low-fat milk

good pinch of saffron threads

4 medium onions

¼ cup canola oil

½ teaspoon hot chili powder

1 cinnamon stick, broken in half

5 cardamom pods, lightly bashed to split

3 cloves

1 teaspoon cumin seeds

1½ cups basmati rice or other long-grain rice

3 cups chicken stock

1 teaspoon garam masala

chopped mint and fresh cilantro leaves, to garnish

salt and freshly ground black pepper

1 In a bowl, stir together the garlic, ginger, cinnamon, turmeric, and yogurt with some black pepper and ¼ teaspoon salt. Add the chicken pieces and stir to coat. Cover and marinate in the refrigerator for about 1 hour or longer, if you have time. Warm the milk to tepid, stir in the saffron, and let steep.

2 Preheat the oven to 400°F. Slice each onion in half lengthwise, reserve half, and cut the other half into thin slices. Pour 1½ tablespoons of the oil onto a baking sheet, sprinkle with the sliced onion over it, toss to coat, then spread out in a thin, even layer. Roast for 40–45 minutes, stirring halfway, until golden.

3 Meanwhile, when the chicken has marinated, thinly slice the reserved onion. Heat 1 tablespoon of the remaining oil in a large sauté pan or skillet. Sauté the onion for 4–5 minutes, until golden brown. Stir in the chicken, a spoonful at a time, cooking until it is no longer opaque, before adding the next spoonful (this helps to prevent the yogurt from curdling). Once the last of the chicken has been added, stir-fry for another 5 minutes. Stir in the chili powder, then pour in ½ cup of water, stir well, cover, and simmer on low heat for 15 minutes. Remove and set aside.

4 Heat another 1 tablespoon of the oil in a large sauté pan, then add the cinnamon stick, cardamoms, cloves, and cumin seeds. Cook briefly until their aroma is released. Add the rice and cook for 1 minute, stirring constantly. Stir in the stock and bring to a boil. Lower the heat and simmer, covered, for about 8 minutes or until all the stock has been absorbed. Remove from the heat and keep covered with the lid for a few minutes so that the rice can fluff up. Stir the garam masala into the remaining oil and set aside. When the onions are roasted, remove and reduce the oven temperature to 350°F.

5 Spoon half of the chicken and its juices into an ovenproof dish, about 10 x 7 x 2½ inches, then sprinkle one-third of the roasted onions over the poultry. Remove the whole spices from the rice, then layer half of the rice over the chicken and onions. Drizzle with the spiced oil. Spoon the rest of the chicken and one-third more onions over the top. Add the remaining rice and drizzle with the saffron-steeped milk. Sprinkle with the rest of the onions, cover tightly with aluminum foil, and heat through in the oven for about 25 minutes. Serve sprinkled with the mint and cilantro.

use canola oil instead of butter or ghee to cut saturated fat

•

choose skinless chicken breasts to reduce the fat

•

use a good balance of spices and herbs to reduce salt

•

Roast onions instead of frying them so that they need less oil

Paella

This Spanish speciality is a harmonious mixture of meat and seafood. The choice of ingredients, however, can all impact on the fat or sodium. I've adjusted to create a recipe that still delivers an authentic taste.

	Classic	Lighter
Kcals	729	609
Fat	25 g	8.6 g
Sat fat	7.5 g	2 g
Sodium	920 mg	760 mg

Per serving 609 kcals

Protein 48.5 g, carbs 77.5 g, fat 8.6 g, sat fat 2g, fiber 6.9 g, sugar 8.5 g, sodium 760 mg

Serves 4

Prep: 25 minutes, plus infusing
Cook: 30 minutes

large pinch of saffron threads, about ¼ teaspoon

7 oz cooked shrimp, in their shells, thawed if frozen

1½ tablespoons olive oil

3 slices prosciutto, trimmed of excess fat, coarsely chopped

1 onion, finely chopped

3 plump garlic cloves, finely chopped

1 lb boneless, skinless chicken breasts, cut into cubes

1 large red bell pepper, cored, seeded, and chopped

1½ teaspoons paprika

½ teaspoon smoked paprika

1¾ cups Spanish paella rice or risotto rice

2½ cups hot chicken stock, from a good-quality bouillon cube

⅔ cup dry white wine

2 tomatoes, coarsely chopped

⅔ cup frozen peas

1 cup trimmed 1 inch fine green bean pieces

handful of chopped flat leaf parsley

salt and freshly ground black pepper

lemon wedges, to serve

1 Stir the saffron into 1 tablespoon hot water and set aside for the flavors to steep while you prepare the paella. Peel the shrimp, leaving the tails on.

2 Heat 1 tablespoon of the oil in a paella pan or large, deep sauté pan. Add the prosciutto and cook for about 1 minute or until crisp. Remove with a slotted spoon, letting any fat drain back into the pan, and set aside. Stir the onion and garlic into the pan and sauté for 4–5 minutes, stirring occasionally. Pour in the remaining ½ tablespoon oil, add the chicken, and stir-fry over medium-high heat for 5 minutes. Stir in the red bell pepper and both paprikas, then the rice. The bottom of the pan should have a lot of brown crispy sediment on it, which will add flavor.

3 Pour in the stock, wine, ⅔ cup of boiling water, and the saffron and its liquid, scraping up the brown sediment from the bottom of the pan. Add the chopped tomatoes, cover, and cook over medium heat for 10 minutes, stirring just occasionally. Sprinkle the peas and shrimp on top, cover again, and cook for another 4–5 minutes or until the rice is just cooked and most of the liquid has been absorbed. Meanwhile, steam the beans for 4–5 minutes, then add them to the pan.

4 Remove from the heat, keep the pan covered, and let the paella stand for 5 minutes. Season to taste with black pepper and a little salt, lightly mix, sprinkle with the parsley and crisp prosciutto, and serve with lemon wedges.

swap chorizo for prosciutto to help lower the fat—and regain any loss of flavor by mixing in smoked paprika powder

DEVILISHLY GOOD DESSERTS

New York cheesecake

A good recipe for this New York classic will capture the necessary qualities of a creamy texture, tangy taste, and the essential seductive ooze in the center—the kind of dessert you can't wait to dig your fork into. This one is much lighter but just as decadent.

	Classic	Lighter
Kcals	665	315
Fat	49 g	15 g
Sat fat	30.2 g	8 g
Sugar	32.6 g	28 g

Per slice 315 kcals

Protein 9 g, carbs 37 g, fat 15 g, sat fat 8 g, fiber 1 g, sugar 28 g, sodium 356 mg

Cuts into 10 slices

Prep: 25 minutes, plus cooling and chilling
Cook: 50 minutes

For the crust

2½ tablespoons butter

¾ cup finely crushed reduced-fat graham crackers

For the filling

2⅔ cups light cream cheese, at room temperature

¾ cup plus 2 tablespoons granulated sugar

3 tablespoons cornstarch

1½ teaspoons finely grated lemon zest

1 teaspoon lemon juice

1 teaspoon vanilla extract

3 extra-large eggs, at room temperature, beaten

⅔ cup fromage blanc or reduced-fat Greek yogurt, or ricotta mixed with plain yogurt

For the topping

2 tablespoons granulated sugar

1½ cups blueberries

½ teaspoon finely grated lime zest

½ cup fromage blanc or reduced-fat Greek yogurt, or ricotta mixed with plain yogurt

1 Preheat the oven to 350°F. Line an 8 inch loose-bottom or springform cake pan with parchment paper and stand it on a baking sheet. Melt the butter in the saucepan and stir in the cookie crumbs. Press the mix into the bottom of the pan, then bake for 10 minutes. Remove from the oven and increase the oven temperature to 475°F.

2 For the filling, beat the cream cheese just until smooth with an electric hand mixer on low speed. Gradually add the sugar, also on low speed, then the cornstarch without overbeating. Scrape the sides of the bowl. Slowly beat in the lemon zest and juice, the vanilla, then the eggs. Scrape the sides of the bowl, then finally beat in the fromage blanc. The mixture should be smooth and runny.

3 Pour the filling over the cookie crust. Shake the pan to level the mixture and squash any surface bubbles with a teaspoon. Bake for 10 minutes, then lower the heat to 225°F. Bake for another 25 minutes and, if you are using an electric oven, keep the oven door slightly ajar for the first 3 minutes. After the 25 minutes, shake the pan; there should be a wobble in the center of the filling. If left until firmer, there will be a greater chance that it may crack later. Turn off the oven, keep the door closed, and let the cake sit in it for 2 hours. Open the door, loosen the top edges of the cake with a blunt knife, then let stand in the oven to cool gently for another 1–1½ hours.

4 Meanwhile, put the sugar for the topping in a small saucepan with 3 tablespoons of water. Bring to a simmer, stirring to dissolve the sugar, then let it simmer for 1–2 minutes to make a thin syrup. Add the blueberries, gently stir, and cook for about 1 minute, just to slightly burst the fruit and release the purple juices. Stir in the lime zest, then let cool.

5 Spread the fromage blanc over the top of the cooled cheesecake. Cover with aluminum foil and chill for at least 4 hours (or overnight). Remove from the refrigerator 1 hour before serving, loosen the sides of the cheesecake completely, remove from the pan, then slide onto a plate, peeling off the paper as you do so. Slice with a sharp knife and serve each wedge topped with a spoonful of the syrupy blueberries.

Reduce fat by making the crust thinner and using reduced-fat crackers

•

use light cream cheese instead of regular and fromage blanc instead of sour cream

•

use whole eggs instead of whole eggs plus extra yolks

•

omit sugar from the crust and reduce it in the filling

Coffee panna cotta

This is one of those desserts that is hard to resist. However, because it is traditionally made with cream and little else, fat levels shoot right up. This version won't disappoint—it's creamy with a silky smooth texture but has far less fat and fewer calories.

	Classic	Lighter
Kcals	591	270
Fat	54.2 g	19.2 g
Sat fat	33.7 g	12.2 g
Sugar	23.4 g	17.7 g

Per serving 270 kcals

Protein 6.4 g, carbs 17.8 g, fat 19.2 g, sat fat 12.2 g, fiber 0g, sugar 17.7 g, sodium 80 mg

Serves 4

Prep: 15 minutes, plus steeping, cooling, and several hours chilling (or overnight chilling)
Cook: 3 minutes

½ cup light whipping cream

¼ cup granulated sugar

½ vanilla bean, halved lengthwise

2 small gelatin sheets, each 4½ x 2½ inches

2 teaspoons instant coffee granules

1 cup Greek yogurt

⅔ cup buttermilk

sifted unsweetened cocoa powder, for dusting

1 Put the cream and sugar into a small saucepan. Scrape in the seeds from the vanilla bean, then drop in the bean. Stir over low heat until the sugar has dissolved. Bring the mixture just to a boil, then remove from the heat and let steep for 5 minutes.

2 Meanwhile, lay the gelatin sheets in a shallow dish and pour over enough cold water to cover them. Let soak for 4–5 minutes.

3 Remove the gelatin sheets from the water, squeeze well to remove the excess water, then stir the sheets into the hot cream until dissolved. Stir in the coffee granules until they are also dissolved. Let the mixture stand until cold, stirring occasionally. Keep checking so that you can catch it before it starts to set. You want it to stay runny.

4 Discard the vanilla bean. Beat the yogurt and buttermilk together in a large bowl, then gradually pour and beat in the cold coffee mixture. Transfer it to a liquid measuring cup and pour into 4 small (⅔ cup) dariole molds. Chill for 4–5 hours or overnight.

5 To loosen when ready to serve, dip each mold into a bowl of hot water (to just below the rim) for only a few seconds. Turn each one out onto a small plate or saucer. Redip if they don't fall out the first time. Lightly dust with cocoa powder.

Replace heavy cream with whipping cream, Greek yogurt, and buttermilk to greatly reduce fat and calories

Chocolate tart

A chocolate tart with a rich taste—but with two-thirds less fat than the classic. You can serve each slice with 1 tablespoon reduced-fat crème fraîche, but the fat will increase to 15.3 g (sat fat 8.6 g) per serving.

	Classic	Lighter
Kcals	542	243
Fat	39.4 g	13.4 g
Sat fat	24.2 g	7.3 g
Sugar	25.1 g	13.7 g

Per slice 243 kcals

Protein 4.4 g, carbs 25.8 g, fat 13.4 g, sat fat 7.3 g, fiber 1.3 g, sugar 13.7 g, sodium 120 mg

Cuts into 8 slices

Prep: 35 minutes, plus chilling and cooling
Cook: 25 minutes

For the pastry dough

1¼ cups all-purpose flour, plus extra for dusting

4 tablespoons butter, cut into pieces

2 teaspoons unsweetened cocoa powder

1 tablespoon confectioners' sugar

1 tablespoon canola oil

1 large egg yolk

For the filling

4 oz bittersweet chocolate, finely chopped

1 tablespoon unsweetened cocoa powder, plus ½ teaspoon for dusting

¾ teaspoon instant coffee granules

½ teaspoon vanilla extract

2 tablespoons low-fat milk

2 large egg whites

2 tablespoons packed dark brown sugar

⅓ cup reduced-fat crème fraîche or Greek yogurt, plus extra to serve (optional)

1 Put the flour into a mixing bowl and remove 2 teaspoons (the cocoa will replace it later). Add the butter and rub into the flour with your fingertips until the mixture resembles fine bread crumbs. Sift in the cocoa and confectioners' sugar, then, using a blunt knife, stir in the oil, egg yolk, and 1½–2 tablespoons of cold water until the dough comes together. Gently gather into a ball, then roll out on a lightly floured surface until large enough to fit a 8 inch round, 1½ inch deep, loose-bottom tart pan. Ease the dough into the pan, leaving a slight overhang. Lightly prick the bottom with a fork, then chill for about 10 minutes.

2 Preheat the oven to 375°F. Place the pan on a baking sheet. Line the pastry dough with parchment and fill with pie weights or dried beans. Bake for 15 minutes or until set. Carefully lift out the weights and paper, then bake the pastry shell for another 10 minutes or until the bottom is cooked. Remove, carefully trim off the overhanging pastry with a sharp knife to give the pastry a flat edge, then let stand until completely cold.

3 To make the filling, put the chocolate in a large heatproof bowl that will fit over a saucepan of simmering water without touching it. Mix the cocoa, coffee, and vanilla with the milk. Pour the mixture over the chocolate. Sit the bowl over the pan of gently simmering water, stir, then immediately remove the pan from the heat, with the bowl of chocolate still over the water, stirring occasionally to check when melted. Stir the melted chocolate—it will be thick. Stir in 2 tablespoons of boiling water and the chocolate will immediately thin down and become silky smooth. Remove the bowl from the pan and let cool slightly.

4 Whisk the egg whites to stiff peaks, then beat in the sugar until thick and glossy. Fold the crème fraîche into the cooled chocolate. Fold one-third of the egg whites into the chocolate mixture, using a large metal spoon, then gently fold in the remaining whites, one-third at a time, until evenly mixed in. Remove the pastry shell from the pan and place on a serving plate. Spoon the filling into the shell, then spread out gently and evenly. Chill for about 3 hours, or overnight, before serving. Serve with a dusting of cocoa and reduced-fat crème fraîche, if you like.

Replace some of the butter in the pastry with canola oil to reduce saturated fat

•

Instead of cream, use less reduced-fat crème fraîche and maintain bulk and texture with whisked egg white

•

Choose a good-quality dark chocolate so that you can use less and keep fat lower. Strengthen the rich taste with a little cocoa powder

Strawberry whip

Crush some ripe strawberries, fold them into a bowlful of sweetened whipped cream, and you have a winning flavor combination for a fruit whip. Strawberries and cream are great partners, but cream makes this a high-fat dessert. By switching ingredients around, I've found other ways to create the desired richness and reduce fat dramatically.

	Classic	Lighter
Kcals	452	169
Fat	40.4 g	9.1 g
Sat fat	25 g	5.8 g
Sugar	20 g	15 g

Per serving 169 kcals

Protein 5.3 g, carbs 15 g, fat 9.1 g, sat fat 5.8 g, fiber 1.8 g, sugar 15 g, sodium 40 mg

Serves 4

Prep: 20 minutes, plus chilling

1 lb 2 oz fresh strawberries, hulled

1 tablespoon plus 1 teaspoon granulated sugar

2 teaspoons crème de cassis

¼ cup light whipping cream

⅔ cup Greek yogurt

⅓ cup reduced-fat crème fraîche or extra Greek yogurt

1 Coarsely chop the strawberries, then coarsely mash together with the sugar and cassis, using a fork if the strawberries are ripe enough, or briefly in a few short bursts using a food processor or immersion blender. Try not to over-process, because it's good to leave a few chunky pieces of fruit.

2 Transfer the strawberries to a fine strainer set over a bowl and let stand for about 10 minutes for the excess juice to drain into it. This makes sure the whip is not too liquidy.

3 Beat the whipping cream in a large bowl to soft peaks, then fold in the yogurt and crème fraîche. Fold in the crushed strawberries and reserve the drained juice. Spoon the strawberry whip into glasses or small bowls and chill for 1–2 hours before serving. Serve with the drained juice.

Use Greek yogurt, reduced-fat crème fraîche, and light whipping cream to replace heavy cream and lower the fat and saturated fat

Fruity sponge cake and custard

One way I found to make this sponge recipe light yet comforting was to layer in more fruit. To simplify the cooking, I switched from steaming the cake traditionally on the stove to "steaming" it in the oven, in a roasting pan with water added.

	Classic	Lighter
Kcals	529	318
Fat	28 g	14 g
Sat fat	16 g	8 g
Sugar	50 g	27 g

Per serving (cake) 318 kcals

Protein 5 g, carbs 45 g, fat 14 g, sat fat 8 g, sugar 27 g, sodium 276 mg

	Classic	Lighter
Kcals	209	115
Fat	14.3 g	7 g
Sat fat	7.2 g	4 g
Sugar	17.5 g	8 g

Per serving (custard) 115 kcals

Protein 3 g, carbs 11 g, fat 7 g, sat fat 4 g, sugar 8 g, sodium 40 mg

Serves 6

Prep: 20 minutes
Cook: 1¼ hours

For the cake

1 large sweet, crisp apple, peeled, cored, and quartered

1 cup fresh or frozen blackberries or raspberries

¼ cup granulated sugar, plus 2 tablespoons

1¼ cups all-purpose flour

1½ teaspoons baking powder

¼ cup firmly packed light brown sugar

6 tablespoons butter, at room temperature, plus extra for greasing

2 extra-large eggs

2 tablespoons low-fat milk

finely grated zest of 1 orange

For the custard

2 tablespoons granulated sugar

1½ teaspoons custard powder or vanilla puddin and pie filling mix

1½ teaspoons cornstarch

1¼ cups low-fat milk

1 extra-large egg yolk

1 vanilla bean

1 cup reduced-fat crème fraîche or Greek yogurt

1 Lightly butter a deep, 1 quart ovenproof baking dish. Preheat the oven to 350°F. Coarsely grate one of the apple quarters and thinly slice the rest. Combine the sliced apple and berries, toss with the 2 tablespoons of granulated sugar, and spoon half into the bottom of the dish.

2 Mix together the flour and baking powder. Beat both the sugars and butter together in a large bowl with an electric hand mixer until light and creamy. Break in 1 egg and beat well, then beat in the second egg (the mixture will look curdled). Sift half of the flour mixture over the sponge mixture and fold in gently. Carefully stir in half of the milk, then repeat with the rest of the flour and milk, followed by the orange zest and reserved grated apple.

3 Spoon two-thirds of the sponge mixture over the fruit mix in the dish and level off. Spread the rest of the fruit on top, followed by the remaining sponge mixture. Place the dish in a small roasting pan filled halfway with hot water. Bake for 1¼ hours (place aluminum foil over the top for the last 15 minutes if it is browning too quickly) or until a toothpick or the tines of a fork inserted in the middle comes out clean.

4 While the cake is baking, make the custard. In a mixing bowl, mix the sugar, custard powder, and cornstarch with 1 tablespoon of the milk to make a paste. Beat in the egg yolk. Pour the remaining milk into a saucepan, halve the vanilla bean lengthwise, and scrape the vanilla seeds into the milk. Add the bean to the milk and bring just to a boil. Pour the milk over the cornstarch paste, stir, then pour into a clean saucepan. Cook over medium heat, stirring all the time, until it is thick enough to coat the back of a spoon. Remove from the heat and stir in the crème fraîche.

5 Loosen the cake from the sides of the dish with a blunt knife and carefully turn it out onto a serving plate. Serve with the custard.

use less butter and fewer eggs in the cake and add low-fat milk to reduce the fat

•

Replace whole milk with low-fat milk in the custard, replace some egg yolks with custard powder and cornstarch and replace cream with reduced-fat crème fraîche to reduce the fat farther

•

Replace some of the sugar in the cake with orange zest and fresh fruit for flavor

Syrupy sponge cakes

Much fat and sugar is used in the classical version of this sponge cake, but with some changes and reductions, I've kept the cake light and moist with just the right balance of sweetness.

	Classic	Lighter
Kcals	540	359
Fat	27.8 g	12.6 g
Sat fat	16.5 g	3.7 g
Sugar	46.9 g	33.1 g

Per cake 359 kcals

Protein 7.4 g, carbs 53.6 g, fat 12.6 g, sat fat 3.7 g, fiber 1.2 g, sugar 33.1 g, sodium 360 mg

Makes 6

Prep: 25 minutes
Cook: 20–25 minutes

¼ cup plus 1 tablespoon light corn syrup

1 small orange (½ teaspoon finely grated zest and 2 tablespoons, plus 1 teaspoon juice)

1⅓ cups flour

1 tablespoon baking powder

½ cup firmly packed light brown sugar

¼ cup ground almonds (almond meal)

2 extra-large eggs

¾ cup plain yogurt

1 teaspoon black molasses

2 tablespoons butter, melted

2 tablespoons canola oil, plus ¼ teaspoon for greasing

1 Preheat the oven to 350°F. Grease six 1-cup metal molds with ¼ teaspoon canola oil, then sit them on a baking sheet. Stir together ¼ cup of the light corn syrup, the orange zest, and the 2 tablespoons orange juice and spoon a little into the bottom of each mold.

2 Put the flour, baking powder, sugar, and ground almonds into a large mixing bowl and make a well in the center. Beat the eggs in a separate bowl, then stir in the yogurt and molasses. Pour this mixture, along with the melted butter and 2 tablespoons oil, into the dry mixture and stir together briefly with a large metal spoon, just so that everything is well combined. Divide the mixture evenly among the molds. Bake for 20–25 minutes or until the desserts have risen to the top of the molds and feel firm.

3 Mix together the remaining 1 tablespoon light corn syrup and 1 teaspoon orange juice to drizzle over the cakes as a sauce. To serve, if the cake tops have peaked slightly, slice off to level so that they sit upright when turned out. Loosen around the sides with a blunt knife, then turn out onto plates. Scrape out any syrupy parts remaining in the molds and put on top of the cakes, then drizzle a little of the syrup sauce over and around each one.

use yogurt and canola oil instead of all butter in the cake mixture to reduce the fat and saturated fat

Tiramisu

This recipe has been one of the the most requested when it comes to tackling a traditional recipe to make lighter. Everyone is concerned about the fat, but there is a lovely creamy taste that needs to stay, so this was about balancing a combination of cheeses and crème fraîche.

	Classic	Lighter
Kcals	442	220
Fat	30.6 g	10.1 g
Sat fat	17.7 g	5.8 g
Sugar	24.9 g	17.4 g

Per serving 220 kcals

Protein 5.7 g, carbs 25.5 g, fat 10.1 g, sat fat 5.8 g, fiber 0.3 g, sugar 17.4 g, sodium 100 mg

Serves 8

Prep: 35 minutes, plus cooling and chilling
Cook: 10 minutes

For the sponge layer

1 cup strong hot coffee, preferably made using freshly ground coffee

1 tablespoon granulated sugar

¼ cup medium red wine

18 ladyfingers

For the filling

1 tablespoon granulated sugar

1 tablespoon cornstarch

⅔ cup low-fat milk

1 large egg

½ vanilla bean, halved lengthwise

⅓ cup reduced-fat crème fraîche or Greek yogurt

1 tablespoon medium red wine

⅔ cup light mascarpone cheese

½ cup light cream cheese

½ teaspoon sifted unsweetened cocoa powder, for dusting

fresh raspberries, to decorate (optional)

1 First make the coffee soaking liquid for the ladyfingers. Stir the coffee and sugar together, then pour into a shallow heatproof dish. Stir in the red wine and let cool.

2 Meanwhile, prepare the filling. Put the sugar and cornstarch into a medium saucepan, preferably nonstick. Stir in 1 tablespoon of the milk to make a thin, smooth paste. Separate the egg, putting the white into a mixing bowl and setting it aside, and dropping the yolk into the saucepan. Beat the yolk into the cornstarch paste, then stir in the rest of the milk. Scrape the seeds from the vanilla bean into the pan, then drop in the bean. Cook over medium-low heat for 8–10 minutes without letting the mixture boil, stirring all the time, until the mixture thickly coats the back of a wooden spoon. Remove from the heat, then stir in the crème fraîche and red wine. Transfer the mixture to a bowl, cover the surface with plastic wrap, and let stand until cold.

3 To assemble, line a 9 x 5 x 2½ inch loaf pan with plastic wrap, leaving an overhang at the top. Beat together the mascarpone and cream cheese, then stir into the rest of the cold filling. Whisk the egg white to stiff peaks and gently fold into the filling, using a large metal spoon.

4 Dip one of the ladyfingers into the coffee mixture, rolling it around briefly, for only a few seconds, to coat and soak in, then lift it out before it has a chance to get too soggy. If left in the coffee, it will disintegrate. Lay it lengthwise in the bottom of the pan. Do the same with another 5 of the ladyfingers, trimming to fit, if necessary, so that they cover the bottom of the pan. Remove the vanilla bean from the filling. Spoon half of the filling over the cookies, spreading it to cover them, then repeat the cookie dipping with another 6 of the ladyfingers. Spoon and spread over the rest of the filling, then dip and lay the rest of the ladyfingers over the top. Bring the plastic wrap overhang over to cover. Chill overnight.

5 To serve, turn out onto a serving plate and carefully peel off the plastic wrap. Dust the top with the cocoa and sprinkle with raspberries, if you like. Slice and serve on the same day.

Reduce egg yolks and sugar by making a low-fat custard instead of a sabayon

•

Swap regular mascarpone for a mixture of light mascarpone and light cream cheese

•

Cut down the amount of mascarpone and extend the filling instead with a whisked egg white

•

Serve smaller portions by making the dessert in a loaf pan, then serving in slices

Lemon tart

This tangy, creamy, rich dessert is particularly hard to alter. However, I've found ways to lower both fat and sugar, yet retain the sweet butteriness of the pastry and the seductive taste of the filling.

	Classic	Lighter
Kcals	323	186
Fat	18 g	9 g
Sat fat	9 g	4 g
Sugar	27 g	15 g

Per serving 186 kcals

protein 4 g, carbs 24 g, fat 9 g, sat fat 4 g, fiber 0 g, sugar 15 g, sodium 56 mg

Cuts into 12 slender slices

Prep: 35 minutes plus chilling
  and standing
Cook: 50–55 minutes

Reduce fat by replacing some of the butter in the pastry with canola oil. Cut down on egg yolks in the filling. Replace cream with reduced-fat crème fraîche

For the pastry dough

4 tablespoons butter, cut into pieces

1¼ cups all-purpose flour, plus extra for dusting

1 tablespoon sifted confectioners' sugar

1 tablespoon extra virgin canola oil

1 large egg yolk

For the filling

3 large eggs, plus 2 large egg whites

1¼ cups confectioners' sugar, plus extra for dusting

2 tablespooons finely grated lemon zest

½ cup lemon juice

1 cup reduced-fat crème fraîche or Greek yogurt

1 In a mixing bowl, rub the butter into the flour with your fingertips until the mixture resembles like fine bread crumbs. Stir in the confectioners' sugar, then make a well and use a blunt knife to stir in the oil, egg yolk, and 1½–2 tablespoons ofcold water until the dough comes together. Without overhandling, gather into a ball. On a lightly floured surface, roll out to fit a deep 9 x ¾ inch, loose-bottom tart pan. Ease the dough into the pan, then trim the edges by rolling the rolling pin over the top. Press the dough into the flutes so that it sits slightly protruding of the edge. Lightly prick the dough bottom with a fork, then chill for about 10 minutes. Preheat the oven to 375°F.

2 Beat the eggs and egg whites together in a mixing bowl with a wooden spoon until well mixed. Sift the confectioners' sugar into a separate bowl, then gradually beat in the eggs. If the mix is lumpy, simply beat with a wire whisk. Stir in the lemon zest and juice. Let stand while you bake the pastry shell so that the lemon flavor can develop.

3 Sit the chilled pastry shell on a baking sheet. Line with parchment paper and pie weights or dried beans and bake for 20 minutes, until well set. Carefully lift out the weights and paper, then bake the pastry shell for another 3–5 minutes, until the pastry is cooked and pale golden.

4 Strain the lemon mixture through a strainer. Beat the crème fraîche in a mixing bowl until smooth, then slowly stir in the lemon mixture until well blended. Transfer to a liquid measuring cup, then carefully pour two-thirds into the warm pastry shell. Place in the oven with the oven shelf half out, pour in the rest of the filling, then carefully slide the shelf back in. Reduce the heat to 300°F. Bake for 25–30 minutes, until set with a slight wobble in the middle. Cool for about an hour, then serve with a light dusting of confectioners' sugar. Best eaten the same day.

Blueberry trifle

In search of the lightest, most voluptuous trifle, I carefully considered each layer to maintain the recipe's elegance. The custard, cake, and fruit layers can be made a day ahead ready for assembling.

	Classic	Lighter
Kcals	713 g	292
Fat	53 g	18 g
Sat fat	28 g	10 g
Sugar	34 g	20 g

Per serving 292 kcals

Protein 8g, carbs 26g, fat 18g, sat fat 10g, fiber 1g, sugar 20g, sodium 112 mg

Serves 8

Prep: 30 minutes plus cooling
  and chilling
Cook: 30 minutes

For the custard

2 tablespoons granulated sugar

2 teaspoons custard powder or instant vanilla pudding and pie filling mix

2½ teaspoons cornstarch

1½ cups low-fat milk

1 extra-large egg yolk

1 vanilla bean, halved lengthwise

1 cup reduced-fat crème fraîche or Greek yogurt

For the cake

canola oil, for greasing

¼ cup granulated sugar

2 extra-large eggs

⅓ cup all-purpose flour

¼ teaspoon baking powder
2 tablespoons wild blueberry "no added sugar" fruit spread

3 tablespoons medium red wine

For the fruit

2 tablespoons granulated sugar

finely grated zest of 1 small lime

1½ cups fresh blueberries

For the topping

1 cup Greek yogurt

1 cup light mascarpone

2 teaspoons granulated sugar

1 First make the custard. In a mixing bowl, blend the sugar, custard powder, and cornstarch with 1 tablespoon of the milk to make a runny paste, then beat in the egg yolk. Pour the remaining milk into a saucepan, scrape in the vanilla seeds, and add the bean, then let come just to a boil. Stir the hot milk into the cornstarch paste, then pour into a clean saucepan. Cook over medium heat, stirring all the time, until thickened. Remove from the heat, then stir in the crème fraîche until smooth. Pour the custard into a bowl, cover the surface with plastic wrap to stop a skin from forming, and let cool, then chill until completely cold.

2 Make the cake. Preheat the oven to 350°F. Lightly grease an 8 inch round cake pan with canola oil, then line the bottom with parchment paper. Put the sugar and eggs into a bowl. Beat with an electric hand mixer for 5 minutes, until the mixture is thick, paler in color, and the consistency of whipped cream. Sift over the flour and baking powder and quickly, but lightly, fold them in. Spoon the batter into the pan and carefully level it, being careful not to squash it. Bake for 25 minutes, until risen, then remove and cool on a wire rack. Peel off the lining paper. Halve the cake so that you have a semicircle. (The other half can be frozen for another time.) Cut the semicircle in half with a knife, then sandwich back together with the fruit spread.

3 Put the sugar and lime zest for the fruit into a saucepan with 2 tablespoons of water. Bring slowly to a boil until the sugar has dissolved, then simmer for 1½–2 minutes, until syrupy. Add the blueberries, then cook briefly, stirring once or twice only, just until they start to burst and release their juices (but still stay whole) and you get a purple syrup. Set aside to cool.

4 The sponge and custard layers can be built up to 2–3 hours ahead of when you want to serve the trifle. Cut the sponge into cubes, then place in the bottom of a glass dish. Drizzle with the red wine. Reserve about one-quarter of the berries for the top, then spoon the rest over the sponge with a little syrup. Discard the bean from the custard, then pour the custard over the fruit.

5 Just before you are ready to serve the trifle, beat together the yogurt, mascarpone, and sugar until smooth and creamy. Pile the mixture onto the custard, then drizzle with the reserved fruit and syrup. Use a toothpick to swirl some of the juices through the creamy topping. Serve immediately, or the syrup will discolor the topping. This is best eaten the same day.

make a fat-free sponge for the cake

•

Reduce the egg yolks in the custard and replace cream with reduced-fat crème fraîche. Use light mascarpone and Greek yogurt for the topping instead of cream

Apple tart

A rich, sweet, and fruity tart in buttery pastry is the perfect way to end a meal. Lowering the fat and sugar that can be hidden between its layers makes this version less of a guilty treat, but the taste satisfaction remains high.

	Classic	Lighter
Kcals	376	260
Fat	19.9 g	11.3 g
Sat fat	13.6 g	5.8 g
Sugar	24.8 g	19.8 g

Per serving 260 kcals

Protein 2.7 g, carbs 31.4 g, fat 11.3 g, sat fat 5.8 g, fiber 4.4 g, sugar 19.8 g, sodium 160 mg

Serves 6

Prep: 35 minutes, plus cooling
Cook: 50 minutes

For the applesauce

3 Pippin or other sweet, crisp apples, cored and coarsely chopped

3 tablespoons apple juice

½ teaspoon vanilla extract

For the pastry dough and topping

1 sheet store-bought puff pastry

all-purpose flour, for dusting

4 Pippin or other sweet, crisp apples, speeled, cored, and thinly sliced

3 teaspoons confectioners' sugar

1 tablespoon apricot preserves

1 Put the apples for the applesauce in a medium saucepan, pour in the apple juice, and simmer, covered, for 20–25 minutes or until really tender, keeping the heat low so that they don't dry out. Remove from the heat, mash with a fork to a rough puree, stir in the vanilla extract, and let cool.

2 Preheat the oven to 425°F. On a lightly floured surface, roll the pastry out to a thin circle, about 13 inches in diameter. Roll the edge over to make a narrow rim, so that you have a circle about 12 inches in diameter. Spread the cooled applesauce over the crust, right up to the rim. Starting from the outside edge and going right up to the rim, arrange the sliced apples for the topping in neat, concentric circles over the applesauce. Sift 2 teaspoons of the confectioners' sugar over the top.

3 Bake for about 20 minutes or until the apples are soft. Sift the rest of the confectioners' sugar over the tart and return to the oven for another 5 minutes so that the apples can start to get tinged brown at the edges.

4 Mix the apricot preserves with 1 tablespoon warm water, then brush it over the baked apple slices and pastry edges to glaze.

cut down on sugar by using sweet, crisp apples—instead of cooking ones—for their natural sweetness

Vanilla ice cream

Good ice cream, by its very nature, is high in fat and sugar. So this recipe required some chemistry wizardry, because sugar stops ice cream from being an ice cube and you need some fat for taste and texture.

	Classic	Lighter
Kcals	285	148
Fat	23 g	8 g
Sat fat	12 g	4 g
Sugar	16.6 g	15 g

Per serving 148 kcals

Protein 4 g, carbs 17 g, fat 8 g, sat fat 4 g, fiber 0 g, sugar 15 g, sodium 44 mg

Makes 8 scoops

Prep: 10 minutes, plus cooling, churning or stirring, and freezing
Cook: 10 minutes

⅓ cup granulated sugar

1½ teaspoons custard powder or instant vanilla pudding and pie filling mix

1½ teaspoons cornstarch

2 cups whole milk

2 extra-large egg yolks

1 vanilla bean, halved lengthwise

1 cup reduced-fat crème fraîche or Greek yogurt

lightly crushed fresh raspberries, to serve

1 Freeze the canister from the ice cream machine in advance if your machine requires you to do so. You can also make this recipe without using a machine.

2 In a mixing bowl, mix the sugar, custard powder, and cornstarch with 2 tablespoons of the milk to make a thin paste. Beat in the egg yolks. Pour the rest of the milk into a saucepan, scrape in the vanilla seeds, and add the bean, then bring to a boil. Pour this slowly over the cornstarch mix, stirring all the time. Clean the pan, then pour the milk mixture and vanilla bean back into it. Cook over medium heat, stirring all the time, until it just comes to a boil and is thick enough to coat the back of a spoon.

3 Remove from the heat, stir in the crème fraîche, then pour into a bowl. Place a piece of plastic wrap over the surface to prevent a skin from forming, then let cool. Chill in the refrigerator until really cold, for at least 4–5 hours but preferably overnight.

4 Remove the vanilla bean from the custard, then transfer the custard to a small bowl. Turn on the ice cream machine, then slowly pour in the custard. Let churn for 10–30 minutes (depending on your machine). When it stops, spoon into a plastic container, cover with plastic wrap and a lid, then freeze for at least 3–4 hours. (If you don't have an ice cream machine, pour the custard into a strong plastic container and freeze for several hours, stirring with a fork once an hour. This will help to give a smoother texture. When almost frozen, freeze for at least 3–4 hours.)

5 For the best results, soften in the refrigerator for 1–1½ hours before serving. Serve with the raspberries. It will keep for up to 1 month. Do not refreeze.

use fewer egg yolks and eliminate heavy cream to reduce the fat and introduce reduced-fat crème fraîche, custard powder, and cornstarch

Chocolate mousse

This sophisticated dessert is great for a dinner party. To serve as a lighter family dessert, you could use an ordinary semisweet chocolate with a lower percentage of cocoa solids, although this will make each serving higher in sugar. This is a favorite for chocaholics, with less than half the fat of a classic recipe.

	Classic	Lighter
Kcals	397	167
Fat	29 g	10 g
Sat fat	14 g	5 g
Sugar	20 g	11 g

Per serving 167 kcals

Protein 4 g, carbs 15g, fat 10 g, sat fat 5g, fiber 2 g, sugar 11 g, sodium 48 mg

Serves 4

Prep: 20 minutes, plus cooling and chilling

3 oz bittersweet chocolate

1 tablespoon unsweetened cocoa powder, plus extra for dusting

½ teaspoon instant coffee granules

½ teaspoon vanilla extract

2 large egg whites

1 tablespoon granulated sugar

¼ cup Greek yogurt

fresh raspberries, to decorate

1 Chop the chocolate finely and put it into a large heatproof bowl that will fit over a saucepan of simmering water. Mix the cocoa, coffee, and vanilla with 2 tablespoons of cold water, and pour the liquid mixture over the chocolate. Place the bowl over the gently simmering water, give it all a stir, then remove from the heat. Keep the bowl of chocolate still over the water, stirring occasionally to check when melted.

2 Stir the melted chocolate—it will be thick. Stir in 2 tablespoons of boiling water and the chocolate will immediately thin down and become silky smooth. Let cool slightly.

3 In a mixing bowl, whisk the egg whites to fairly soft peaks, then beat in the sugar until thick and glossy.

4 Beat the yogurt into the cooled chocolate. Fold about one-third of the egg whites into the chocolate mixture, using a large metal spoon, then gently fold in the rest of the whites until they are evenly mixed in; be careful not to overmix or you will lose the volume of the mousse. Spoon into 4 small cups or ½–⅔ cup ramekins and chill for a couple of hours, or overnight.

5 Place each mousse on a saucer or small plate. Top with a few raspberries, then dust with a little cocoa powder. The mousse will keep for up to 2 days in the refrigerator.

Reduce fat by eliminating egg yolks, butter and cream and by replacing a little of the chocolate with cocoa powder and using Greek yogurt

Apple and blackberry crisp

Like many desserts that are full of fruit, the popular fruit crisp can seem like a healthy option, but it has other ingredients that are high in fat and sugar. By making a few simple changes that don't compromise the taste, the sugar and fat have been lowered considerably.

	Classic	Lighter
Kcals	493	353
Fat	21.6 g	11.9 g
Sat fat	9.5 g	3.2 g
Sugar	45.1 g	33.7 g

Per serving 353 kcals

Protein 5.9 g, carbs 54.1 g, fat 11.9 g, sat fat 3.2 g, fiber 6.5 g, sugar 33.7 g, sodium 40 mg

Serves 5

Prep: 35 minutes
Cook: 35 minutes

For the crisp

⅔ cup all-purpose flour

3 tablespoons ground almonds

½ cup rolled oats

2 tablespoons butter, at soft room temperature, cut into pieces

3 tablespoons granulated sugar

1 teaspoon ground cinnamon

1 tablespoon chopped, toasted hazelnuts

1½ tablespoons canola oil

For the fruit

2 oranges

1 tablespoon demerara sugar or other raw sugar

5 Pippin or other sweet, crisp apples (about 1¾ lb), peeled, cored, and chopped into small chunks

1¼ cups fresh blackberries

1 tablespoon cornstarch

1   Make the crisp topping. Put the flour, ground almonds, oats, and butter into a mixing bowl. Rub the butter in with your fingertips to create coarse bread crumbs. Stir in the sugar, cinnamon, and hazelnuts, then stir in the oil and mix in with your fingers to evenly distribute. Set aside. Preheat the oven to 375°F.

2   Finely grate 1 teaspoon zest from one of the oranges and set aside, then squeeze the juice from both to produce ½ cup of juice. Make up with water, if necessary. Put the orange juice and sugar in a saucepan and simmer for about 1 minute to dissolve the sugar and make it a little syrupy.

3   Add the apples, reserved orange zest, and ¼ cup of water, then simmer for 5 minutes or until the apples are only just starting to soften (they will finish cooking in the oven). Stir in the blackberries and simmer for another 1–2 minutes to release their juices and color the liquid. Stir in the cornstarch, letting the mixture simmer briefly to thicken and make a sauce. Adjust with a little extra water if you want the saucy any thinner.

4   Spoon the fruit into an ovenproof dish, about 10 x 8 x 2 inches, and sprinkle the topping over the fruit, but do not press it down; keep it light and crumbly. Bake for about 25 minutes or until the topping is golden and the fruit and its juices are bubbling up around the edges. Remove and let stand to settle for 10–15 minutes before serving.

create flavor and crunch in the crisp with cinnamon and a few nuts instead of extra sugar. To improve fiber content, include oats to replace some of the flour

Semifreddo with summer fruits

To make sure the texture of this delicious dessert isn't lost, I've adapted both method and ingredients to recreate that same sense of luxurious richness, but in a much lighter way.

	Classic	Lighter
Kcals	322	162
Fat	27.5 g	9 g
Sat fat	15.7 g	5.6 g
Sugar	15 g	13.9 g

Per serving 162 kcals

Protein 4.4 g, carbs 15.7 g, fat 9 g,
sat fat 5.6 g, fiber 1.8 g, sugar 13.9 g,
sodium 40 mg

Serves 8

Prep: 30 minutes, plus cooling,
   chilling, and freezing
Cook: 8 minutes

¼ cup granulated sugar

1½ teaspoons custard powder or instant
vanilla pudding and pie filling mix

1½ teaspoons cornstarch

1 cup whole milk

1 extra-large egg yolk

1 cup reduced-fat crème fraîche
or half-and-half

¼ teaspoon vanilla extract

1 cup Greek yogurt

3½ cups frozen berries, such as hulled
halved or quartered strawberries,
raspberries, and blackberries

2 teaspoons confectioners' sugar

1 Mix the sugar, custard powder, and cornstarch in a mixing bowl with 2 tablespoons of the milk. Beat in the egg yolk. Pour the rest of the milk into a saucepan and bring just to a boil. Pour the hot milk slowly over the cornstarch mix, stirring constantly. Pour this into a clean saucepan, preferably nonstick, and cook over medium heat, stirring all the time with a wooden spoon, until the mixture comes just to a boil, thickens, and coats the back of the spoon—in about 5 minutes. Remove from the heat, stir in the crème fraîche and vanilla, and pour into a bowl. Cover with a piece of plastic wrap and let cool. When it's cooled down, put in the refrigator overnight.

2 Line the bottom of an 8½ x 5 x 2½ inch loaf pan with parchment paper. Spoon the cold custard into a food processor with the yogurt and 2½ cups of the frozen fruit. Process briefly to combine everything and break down the fruit a little. It's important that the fruit is still frozen, because this will also start to freeze the whole mixture. Pour or spoon the mixture into the lined pan, cover, and put in the freezer for about 6 hours. Transfer the rest of the fruit to a strainer set over a small bowl and let thaw and drain.

3 When the rest of the fruit has thawed, set a small handful of the fruit aside for decoration and press the rest through the strainer to make a fruit coulis. Stir in the confectioners' sugar to sweeten. (If your mix of fruit is tart, you may need a pinch more confectioners' sugar.) Refrigerate until ready to serve.

4 To serve, when the semifreddo feels firm enough to turn out but not completely solid, loosen the edges with a small spatula (or dip the pan briefly in hot water to loosen the sides first if that's easier), then turn it out onto a serving plate and peel off the lining paper. Sprinkle the whole fruits down the center and spoon a little of the coulis over them. Serve in slices with the rest of the coulis.

Lower the fat by reducing
the number of eggs and
create texture by making a
lower-fat custard instead

Bread and butter pudding

This traditional British dessert has become richer over the years as well as more fattening. So I've reinvented it to make it lighter by a careful choice of ingredients and using a good amount of fruit.

	Classic	Lighter
Kcals	569	312
Fat	33.8 g	11.5 g
Sat fat	18.1 g	6.1 g
Sugar	33.3 g	19.8 g

Per serving 312 kcals

Protein 9.6 g, carbs 40.9 g, fat 11.5 g, sat fat 6.1 g, fiber 1.7 g, sugar 19.8 g, sodium 332 mg

Serves 4

Prep: 25 minutes, plus soaking
   and steeping
Cook: 30–35 minutes

⅓ cup chopped dried apricots

3 tablespoons raisins

2 tablespoons brandy

1 extra-large egg

1 teaspoon granulated sugar

2 teaspoons custard powder or instant vanilla pudding and pie filling mix

1½ cups low-fat milk

½ vanilla bean, halved lengthwise

zest of 1 small lemon, pared off in strips with a vegetable peeler

¼ cup reduced-fat crème fraîche or Greek yogurt

2 tablespoons butter, at room temperature

4 medium slices good white bread, crusts left on, such as sliced from a small white country-style loaf

1 tablespoon apricot preserves or jam

¼ teaspoon confectioners sugar, sifted, for dusting

1 Put the apricots and raisins in a small dish, pour the brandy over them, and let soak, stirring occasionally.

2 Meanwhile, beat the egg and granulated sugar together in a mixing bowl, then whisk in the custard powder until smooth. Warm the milk in a small, nonstick saucepan, then, when it's just coming to a boil, remove from the heat and slowly stir into the egg mixture. Scrape in the vanilla seeds, add the lemon zest and vanilla bean, and set aside to cool and steep for 30 minutes. Whisk the crème fraîche into the cooled custard, then strain into a bowl.

3 Using ¼ teaspoon of the butter, lightly butter a shallow ovenproof dish, about 8 x 10 x 2 inches.

4 Butter the bread on only one side with the rest of the butter, then spread over the preserves or jam. Cut each slice into 4 triangles, then lay half the triangles, preserves side up, in the dish. Sprinkle with half of the apricots and raisins, then lay the rest of the bread over the top, preserves side up. Sprinkle with the rest of the dried fruit and any unsoaked brandy, then pour half of the custard over the bread. Let soak for 15 minutes. Preheat the oven to 350°F.

5 Place the dish in a roasting pan. Pour the rest of the custard over the bread, press the bread lightly into the custard, then fill the roasting pan halfway with hot water. Bake for 20 minutes, then increase the oven temperature to 375°F and bake for another 5–10 minutes, until the bread on top is crisp and golden. Remove and let the dessert sit for 2–3 minutes. Dust with the confectioners' sugar and serve warm.

use low-fat milk instead of whole, and reduced-fat crème fraîche instead of cream. maintain the flavor by adding lemon, vanilla, and brandy

Strawberry ice cream milk shake

It's hard to refuse a cool, frothy milk shake on a hot day, especially with the added allure of scoops of rich vanilla ice cream blended through it. But with this allure comes a lot of fat and sugar. If you keep a batch of the Vanilla Ice Cream (see p. 144) in the freezer, it's quick to whisk these up as an equally alluring, but low-fat, dessert alternative.

	Classic	Lighter
Kcals	408	196
Fat	19.2 g	7.7 g
Sat fat	12 g	4.6 g
Sugar	47 g	22.8 g

Per glass 196 kcals

Protein 7.7 g, carbs 23.6 g, fat 7.7 g, sat fat 4.6 g, fiber 1.8 g, sugar 22.8 g, sodium 80 mg

Fills 2 tall glasses

Prep: 10 minutes (not including making the ice cream)

1⅔ cups hulled and halved or quartered ripe, fresh strawberries

1 cup low-fat milk

2 tablespoons plain yogurt

2 scoops Vanilla Ice Cream (see recipe p. 144)

1 Put the strawberries in a blender or food processor (or use an immersion blender) with the milk, yogurt, and ice cream, then process until the mixture is creamy and frothy.

2 Pour into 2 tall glasses and spoon the frothy bubbles on top.

Eliminate sugar by using ripe, seasonal strawberries when they are at their natural sweetest

Raspberry and passion fruit meringue

I've tweaked the size of the meringue, generously filled it with lower fat creaminess, and now this recipe is lower in sugar and dramatically lower in fat and calories—yet it still looks and tastes like an indulgence.

	Classic	Lighter
Kcals	326	180
Fat	20.3 g	7.3 g
Sat fat	12.6 g	4.6 g
Sugar	33 g	23.3 g

Per serving 180 kcals

Protein 4.8 g, carbs 23.5 g, fat 7.3 g, sat fat 4.6g, fiber 1.5g, sugar 23.3g, sodium 40 mg

Serves 8

Prep: 25 minutes, plus drying out
Cook: 1 hour

For the meringue

1 teaspoon cornstarch

1 teaspoon white wine vinegar

½ teaspoon vanilla extract

3 extra-large egg whites

½ cup superfine sugar

⅓ cup confectioners' sugar

For the filling

½ cup light whipping cream

1 cup 2% Greek yogurt

⅓ cup reduced-fat crème fraîche or extra Greek yogurt

2 teaspoons superfine sugar

1 passion fruit

3 cups fresh raspberries

1 Preheat the oven to 300°F. Line a large baking sheet with parchment paper and draw an 8 inch circle in pencil in the center of the paper. For the meringue, mix together the cornstarch, vinegar, and vanilla and set aside.

2 Beat the egg whites in a large mixing bowl until the mixture stands in stiff peaks when the beaters are lifted. Start to add the superfine sugar a tablespoon at a time, beating for a few seconds before adding the next tablespoon. (To use granulated sugar instead, first blend an equal amount in a food processor for 1 minute.) When all the superfine sugar has been added, you should have a thick, glossy mixture. Now sift and gently fold in half of the confectioners' sugar, using a large metal spoon. Repeat with the remaining confectioners' sugar, being careful not to overmix. Fold in the cornstarch mixture.

3 Spoon and gently spread the mixture into the circle on the parchment paper, building the sides up slightly so that they are just a little higher. Bake for 1 hour, after which the meringue should sound crisp when gently tapped. Turn the oven off, but keep the meringue inside for another 1 hour to finish drying out as it cools. Don't worry if it cracks a bit; it's part of its character.

4 When ready to serve, remove the merigue shell from the parchment paper and place on a serving plate. Beat the whipping cream for the filling to soft peaks, enough so that it holds its shape. Fold in the yogurt, then the crème fraîche and sugar. Cut the passion fruit in half widthwise, scoop out the pulp and seeds from one half, and lightly ripple through the creamy mixture. Spoon it into the meringue shell. Sprinkle the raspberries on top, drizzling the remaining passion fruit over the meringue as you work. Serve immediately. If left filled for too long, the meringue will start to soften.

Replace most of the cream with 2% Greek yogurt and reduced-fat crème fraîche to greatly reduce fat

Crème brûlée

A winning dessert, this crème brûlée cheats on fat content by using light cream instead of heavy and a custard with fewer eggs. The secret to this healthier version is to initially make sure the custard is made thick, because unlike your classic crème brûlée recipe, the custard won't be baked afterward.

	Classic	Lighter
Kcals	700	257
Fat	65.1 g	14.9 g
Sat fat	38.1 g	8.7 g
Sugar	22 g	18.9 g

Per serving 257 kcals

Protein 5.2 g, carbs 25.3 g, fat 14.9 g, sat fat 8.7 g, sugar 18.9 g, sodium 80 mg

Serves 4

Prep: 15 minutes, plus cooling
and chilling
Cook: 25 minutes

¼ cup granulated sugar

1 tablespoon custard powder or instant vanilla pudding and pie filling mix

1 tablespoon cornstarch

1 cup low-fat milk

2 extra-large egg yolks

½ cup cream

1 vanilla bean

⅔ cup reduced-fat créme fraîche or Greek yogurt

1 Mix 2 tablespoons of the sugar, the custard powder, and cornstarch in a mixing bowl with 2 tablespoons of the milk to make a smooth paste. Beat the egg yolks in well with a fork.

2 Pour the rest of the milk into a saucepan, preferably nonstick, then pour in the cream. Halve the vanilla bean lengthwise and scrape the seeds into the milk. Drop the bean into the pan and bring the creamy milk just to a boil. Remove from the heat as soon as you see a few bubbles rising to the surface.

3 Slowly pour and stir the hot milk into the cornstarch mix, including the vanilla bean, making sure the yolks are well blended in. Transfer to a clean saucepan. Cook over low heat, stirring all the time with a wooden spoon, for 12–15 minutes, until the mixture is thick. When you drag the spoon across the bottom of the pan, it should leave a clean line. The mixture should have thickened after 10 minutes, but keep stirring until it has thickened enough to look like softly whipped cream or mayonnaise. Keep adjusting the heat to prevent the mixture from coming to a boil or overheating, or it may curdle and become lumpy. If this happens, beat smooth with a wire whisk.

4 Remove from the heat and let cool for 15–20 minutes, stirring occasionally to prevent a skin from forming. Remove the vanilla bean. Stir in the créme fraîche and spoon the mixture into 4 small ⅔ cup ramekins. Spread the mixture level, then chill, uncovered, for 4 hours or overnight. By not covering them, a thin skin can form on top of the brûlées, which will help support the caramel layer later.

5 When ready to serve, spoon the remaining sugar over the top of each brûlée (allow 1½ teaspoons per ramekin) and smooth it over with the back of the spoon. To caramelize it, use a kitchen blowtorch. Hold the flame just above the sugar and keep it moving around and around until evenly caramelized, but not too long or the custard will heat up too much. Serve immediately while the caramel is firm and brittle, because it will soften on standing.

make a thick custard that does not require as many egg yolks to set as it would if baked

Caramel date cakes

This dessert is all about excess and naughtiness—but I've discovered that you really don't need all that butter, cream, syrup, sugar, and molasses to make it taste gorgeous.

	Classic	Lighter
Kcals	699	450
Fat	36 g	17.5 g
Sat fat	20.7 g	4.6 g
Sugar	74.4 g	49.8 g

Per serving 450 kcals

Protein 6 g, carbs 70.6 g, fat 17.5 g, sat fat 4.6 g, fiber 2 g, sugar 49.8 g, sodium 316 mg

Makes 7

Prep: 35 minutes, plus cooling
Cook: 20–25 minutes

For the cakes

8 pitted whole dates

1 teaspoon vanilla extract

1 teaspoon black molasses

2 large eggs

1 teaspoon baking soda

1⅓ cups all-purpose flour, plus extra for dusting

1¼ teaspoons baking powder

⅓ cup canola oil, plus ½ teaspoon for greasing

½ cup demerara sugar or other raw sugar

½ cup plain yogurt

For the caramel sauce

½ cup firmly packed light brown sugar

2 tablespoons butter, cut into pieces

1½ teaspoons black molasses

1½ teaspoons vanilla extract

½ cup reduced-fat crème fraîche or Greek yogurt

1 Chop the dates, put them in a small bowl, then pour over ¾ cup of boiling water. Let cool for about 30 minutes. Grease seven 1 cup metal dessert molds with ½ teaspoon oil, then flour and place on a baking sheet.

2 Stir the vanilla extract and molasses into the dates, and mash with a fork to a coarse puree.

3 Preheat the oven to 350° F. To make the cakes, beat the eggs in a small bowl. Mix together the flour, baking powder, and baking soda. Stir the ⅓ cup of oil and the sugar together in a larger mixing bowl, using a wooden spoon. Pour in the eggs a little at a time, beating as you work. Gently fold in one-third of the flour mixture with a large metal spoon, then half of the yogurt. Don't overmix. Repeat, finishing with the last of the flour. Gently stir in the mashed dates in to form a thick batter. Spoon the batter evenly between the molds. Bake for 20–25 minutes.

4 Meanwhile, make the sauce. Put the sugar and butter into a small, heavy saucepan. Heat over low-medium heat, stirring occasionally, until the sugar starts to dissolve, without bringing to a boil. The mixture will be thick and the sugar won't dissolve completely at this stage. Remove the pan from the heat, then stir in the molasses and vanilla. Cool for 1–2 minutes, then stir in the crème fraîche, a spoonful at a time. Use a small wire whisk to make the mixture smooth, if necessary.

5 To serve, loosen around the sides of the cakes with a blunt knife, then turn out onto plates. Spoon and drizzle a little sauce over and around each one.

Reduce the sugar and concentrate the flavor by using unrefined sugar and black molasses, together with vanilla extract

GUILT-FREE BAKING

Carrot cake

Although this American classic is plumped up with freshly grated carrot and blended with oil instead of butter, it's not enough to warrant the healthy tag unless you adjust the ingredients and techniques.

	Classic	Lighter
Kcals	327	217
Fat	20.5 g	9 g
Sat fat	5.5 g	1 g
Sugar	21.5 g	21 g

Per square 217 kcals

Protein 4 g, carbs 31 g, fat 9 g, sat fat 1 g, fiber 2 g, sugar 21 g, sodium 208 mg

Cuts into 16 squares

Prep: 30 minutes, plus soaking
Cook: 1 hour

For the cake

1 medium orange

1 cup raisins

1 cup all-purpose white flour

1 cup whole-wheat flour

2 teaspoons baking powder, plus a pinch

1 teaspoon baking soda

1 teaspoon ground cinnamon

2 extra-large eggs

⅔ cup firmly packed dark brown sugar

½ cup canola oil, plus extra for greasing

2½ cups finely grated carrot

For the frosting

½ light cream cheese, chilled

½ cup quark cheese or Greek yogurt

3 tablespoons confectioners' sugar, sifted

½ teaspoon finely grated orange zest

1½ teaspoons lemon juice

1 Preheat the oven to 325°F. Lightly grease the bottom of a deep 8 inch square cake pan with canola oil, then line the bottom with parchment paper.

2 To make the cake, finely grate the zest from the orange and squeeze 3 tablespoons of the juice. Pour the juice over the raisins in a bowl, stir in the zest, then let soak. Mix the flours with the 1 teaspoon baking powder, the baking soda, and cinnamon.

3 Separate one of the eggs. Put the white in a small bowl and the yolk in a large mixing bowl. Break the remaining egg in with the yolk, then add the sugar. Beat together for 1–2 minutes, until thick and foamy. Slowly pour in the oil and continue to beat on a low speed until well mixed. Add the flour mix, half at a time, and gently stir it into the egg mixture. The mixture will be stiff. Put the extra pinch of baking powder in with the egg white and beat to soft peaks.

4 Fold the carrot and raisins (with any liquid) into the flour mixture. Gently fold in the beaten egg white, then pour into the pan. Shake the pan to level the mixture. Bake for 1 hour, until risen and firm or until a toothpick inserted in the center comes out clean. Let cool in the pan for 5 minutes, turn out onto a wire rack, peel off the lining paper, then let stand until cold.

5 To make the frosting, stir the cream cheese, quark, confectioners' sugar, and orange zest together; don't overbeat. Stir in the lemon juice. Swirl the frosting over the cake and cut into 16 squares. This cake is even better if left for a day or two, well wrapped, before frosting.

Use canola oil, light cream cheese and quark to lower the fats. Reduce sugar in the frosting, and add flavor with oranges and lemons

Chocolate brownies

A brownie can appear in many guises: plump and gooey, nutty, cakey, or fudgy. But it is always exceedingly rich with a thin, crusty top and dark, chewy center. Because this is achieved by mixing together generous combinations of butter, sugar, chocolate, and eggs, my challenge was to create a lighter version that was still irresistible.

	Classic	Lighter
Kcals	314	191
Fat	19 g	11 g
Sat fat	10 g	3 g
Sugar	25.6 g	16 g

Per square 191 kcals

Protein 2 g, carbs 23 g, fat 11 g, sat fat 3 g, fiber 1 g, sugar 16 g, sodium 112 mg

Cuts into 12 squares

Prep: 25 minutes
Cook: 35 minutes

3 oz bittersweet chocolate, chopped into small pieces

canola oil, for greasing

⅔ cup all-purpose flour

¼ cup unsweetened cocoa powder

¼ teaspoon baking soda

½ cup granulated sugar

¼ cup firmly packed light brown sugar

½ teaspoon instant coffee granules

1 teaspoon vanilla extract

2 tablespoons buttermilk

1 extra-large egg

½ cup mayonnaise

1. Preheat the oven to 350°F. Pour enough water into a small saucepan to fill it by one-third. Bring to a boil, then remove the pan from the heat. Put the chopped chocolate into a large heatproof bowl that fits snugly over the pan without touching the water. Sit the pan over the water (still off the heat) and leave the chocolate to melt slowly for a few minutes, stirring occasionally until it has melted evenly. Remove the bowl from the pan, then let the chocolate cool slightly.

2. Meanwhile, lightly grease a 7½ inch square, 2 inch deep cake pan with the canola oil, then line the bottom with parchment paper. Sift together the flour, cocoa, and baking soda. Using a wooden spoon, stir both the sugars into the cooled chocolate with the coffee, vanilla, and buttermilk. Stir in 1 tablespoon warm water. Break and beat in the egg, then stir in the mayonnaise just until smooth and glossy. Sift the flour and cocoa mix over the mixture, then gently fold in with a spatula without overmixing.

3. Pour the batter into the pan, then gently and evenly spread it into the corners. Bake for 30 minutes. When a toothpick is inserted into the middle, it should come out with just a few moist crumbs sticking to it. If cooked too long, the batter will dry out; not long enough and it can sink. Let stand in the pan until completely cold, then loosen the sides with a blunt knife. Turn out onto a board, peel off the lining paper, and cut into 12 squares.

Reduce the fat by replacing all the butter and some of the egg with mayonnaise. Use good-quality chocolate so that you can use less, and intensify the chocolate taste with cocoa powder and coffee granules

Coffee and walnut cake

Walnuts contain a good fat, but they are fattening in terms of calories, so this cake uses alternatives to boost the taste. I've also used coffee syrup livened up with a splash of vanilla to deepen the coffee experience, and abandoned the traditional cake-making method for one that allows me to lighten this coffee-time favorite.

	Classic	Lighter
Kcals	462	336
Fat	27 g	15 g
Sat fat	13 g	4 g
Sugar	42 g	30 g

Per slice 336 kcals

Protein 8 g, carbs 45 g, fat 15 g, sat fat 4 g, fiber 1 g, sugar 30 g, sodium 172 mg

Cuts into 12 slices

Prep: 30 minutes, plus cooling and setting
Cook: 45–50 minutes

For the cake

1 tablespoon instant coffee granules, plus 1 teaspoon

1¾ cups all-purpose flour

2¾ teaspoons baking powder

½ cup ground almonds (almond meal)

⅓ cup firmly packed light brown sugar

¼ cup granulated sugar

¼ cup chopped walnuts

2 extra-large eggs, beaten

1 cup plain yogurt

⅓ cup walnut oil, plus extra for greasing

For the filling

2 tablespoons granulated sugar

2 teaspoons instant coffee granules

⅔ cup light mascarpone cheese

½ cup quark cheese or Greek yogurt

1 tablespoon confectioners' sugar, sifted

¼ teaspoon vanilla extract

For the icing

1¼ cups confectioners' sugar

1 teaspoon instant coffee granules

1 tablespoon finely chopped walnuts

1 Preheat the oven to 350°F. Lightly oil an 8 inch round, 2½ inch deep, loose-bottom cake pan with walnut oil, then line the bottom with parchment paper.

2 For the cake, mix the coffee with 2 teaspoons warm water and set aside. Put the flour into a large mixing bowl. Stir in the baking powder, ground almonds, both sugars, and walnuts, then make a well in the center. Put the eggs, yogurt, oil, and coffee mix into the well and stir the mixture with a wooden spoon so that everything is evenly mixed.

3 Spoon the batter into the prepared pan, smooth the top to level it, then bake for 40–45 minutes, or until a toothpick inserted into the center of the cake comes out clean. Let the cake cool in the pan briefly, then turn it out and peel off the lining paper. Place on a wire rack to cool completely while you make the filling and icing.

4 Make the syrup for the filling. Put the granulated sugar and coffee into a small, heavy saucepan, then pour in 3 tablespoons of water. Heat gently, stirring to help the sugar dissolve. Once dissolved, raise the heat, then boil at a fast rolling boil for 2½–3 minutes, until thickened and syrupy. Pour into a small heatproof bowl and set aside to cool. When cold, it should be the consistency of molasses.

5 Meanwhile, beat together the mascarpone, quark, confectioners' sugar, and vanilla until smooth, then stir in the cold coffee syrup. Set aside.

6 For the icing, sift the confectioners' sugar into a bowl. Mix the coffee with 1 tablespoon of warm water, then stir this into the confectioners' sugar with a little extra water, if necessary, to create a smooth, thick but spreadable icing.

7 Slice the cake into 3, then sandwich back together with the filling. Spread the icing over the top, sprinkle with the chopped walnuts, and let set. Store in the refrigerator.

Replace butter in the cake with walnut oil and yogurt to reduce the fat and saturated fat

•

Replace a buttercream filling with one made with light mascarpone and quark to reduce the fat farther

•

Reduce walnuts and gain walnut flavor from the oil

•

Use less sugar in the cake—bump up the flavor by combining light brown with granulated. Make a filling that requires less sugar

Shoofly pie

With less than half the sugar of a classic shoofly pie, this recipe is bound to impress. By finding ways to reduce the syrup, this is the perfect way to finish a heavy dinner that is far less heavy on the calories. Serve the tart while still warm and, if there is any left, it is equally delicious cold.

	Classic	Lighter
Kcals	469	247
Fat	14.8 g	10.2 g
Sat fat	8.7 g	3.9 g
Sugar	47.9 g	20.1 g

Per slice 247 kcals

Protein 3.6 g, carbs 34.7 g, fat 10.2 g, sat fat 3.9 g, fiber 1.1 g, sugar 20.1 g, sodium 200 mg

Serves 8

Prep: 15 minutes, plus chilling and standing
Cook: 50 minutes

For the crust

1 sheet store-bought rolled dough pie crust, thawed if frozen

all-purpose flour for dusting

For the filling

1 large egg

3 tablespoons reduced-fat crème fraîche or Greek yogurt

¾ cup light corn syrup

1 tablespoon black molasses

1 small Pippin or other sweet, crisp apple, cored, peeled, and grated

1 cup fresh white bread crumbs

1 lemon

Reduce sugar by replacing some of the syrup with grated apple, and use a large egg and reduced-fat crème fraîche to provide bulk and texture

1 Preheat the oven to 400°F. Roll the dough out thinly on a lightly floured surface and use to line a 9 inch round, 1 inch deep, fluted tart pan, easing the dough into the pan and the flutes carefully to prevent it from stretching. Run a rolling pin over the top of the pan to trim off any excess dough. Prick the bottom of the dough lightly with a fork. Chill for 10 minutes.

2 Place the tart pan on a baking sheet. Line the dough with aluminum foil and pie weights or dried beans and bake for 12 minutes, until the pastry is set. Remove the foil and weights from the pastry shell and bake for another 5 minutes, until the pastry is pale golden. Remove and lower the oven temperature to 350°F.

3 While the pastry is baking, make the filling. Beat the egg in a mixing bowl, then stir in the crème fraîche, corn syrup, molasses, grated apple, and bread crumbs. Finely grate the zest from the lemon and stir it into the filling. Mix with 1 tablespoon of squeezed lemon juice. Let stand for 10–15 minutes so that the bread can absorb the other ingredients slightly.

4 Pour the filling into the pastry shell and bake for 30 minutes or until the filling is softly set. Remove the tart and let it cool a little until firm. Remove from the pan and serve.

Lemon drizzle cake

A moist, fragrant slice of lemon drizzle cake is a classic afternoon treat. For this healthier version, I've made a butterless cake and added a lot of lemon zest to the mixture for a really zingy taste.

	Classic	Lighter
Kcals	335	243
Fat	17.9 g	10.2 g
Sat fat	10.4 g	1.4 g
Sugar	27.6 g	21.5 g

Per slice 243 kcals

Protein 4.7 g, carbs 35.4 g, fat 10.2 g, sat fat 1.4 g, fiber 0.9 g, sugar 21.5 g, sodium 136 mg

Cuts into 12 slices

Prep: 25 minutes
Cook: 40 minutes

For the cake

1⅓ cups all-purpose flour

1 tablespoon baking powder

½ cup ground almonds (almond meal)

⅓ cup cornmeal

finely grated zest of 2 lemons

¾ cup granulated sugar

2 extra-large eggs

1 cup plain yogurt

⅓ cup canola oil, plus extra for greasing

For the syrup

⅓ cup granulated sugar

juice of 2 lemons (about ⅓ cup)

1 Preheat the oven to 350°F). Lightly grease an 8 inch round, 2 inch deep cake pan with canola oil, then line the bottom with parchment paper.

2 For the cake, put the flour, baking powder, ground almonds, and cornmeal in a large mixing bowl. Stir in the lemon zest and sugar, then make a well in the center. Beat the eggs in a bowl, then stir in the yogurt. Add this mixture along with the oil into the well, then briefly and gently stir with a large metal spoon so that everything is just combined, without overmixing.

3 Spoon the batter into the pan and level the top. Bake for 40 minutes or until a toothpick inserted into the center of the cake comes out clean. Cover loosely with aluminum foil for the final 5–10 minutes if it starts to brown too quickly.

4 While the cake cooks, make the lemon syrup. Put the sugar into a small saucepan with the lemon juice and ⅓ cup of water. Heat over medium heat, stirring occasionally, until the sugar has dissolved. Raise the heat, boil for 4 minutes, until slightly reduced and syrupy, then remove from the heat.

5 Remove the cake from the oven and let it cool briefly in the pan. While it is still warm, turn it out of the pan, peel off the lining paper, and sit the cake on a wire rack set over a baking sheet or plate. Use a toothpick to make a lot of small holes all over the top of the cake. Slowly spoon over half of the lemon syrup and let it soak in. Spoon the rest over the cake in the same way, brushing the edges and sides of the cake too with the last of the syrup.

Mix in ground almonds to lighten and moisten, and bulk out with cornmeal, which intensifies the texture and color

Sticky gingerbread

Most people's favorite kind of gingerbread is moist, sticky, and dark. To gain these qualities, a lot of butter, sugar, syrup, and milk is involved. Here, I've kept the characteristics with less fat and sugar. If you keep the cake well wrapped for a day before cutting, you'll find it gets even stickier.

	Classic	Lighter
Kcals	162	130
Fat	6.9 g	4 g
Sat fat	4 g	1.1 g
Sugar	13 g	11 g

Per square 130 kcals

Protein 2.3 g, carbs 21.1 g, fat 4 g, sat fat 1.1 g, fiber 0.6 g, sugar 11 g, sodium 120 mg

Cuts into 16 squares

Prep: 25 minutes, plus cooling
Cook: about 55 minutes

6 dried pitted whole dates, chopped into small pieces

2 tablespoons butter

¼ cup black molasses

2 tablespoons light corn syrup syrup

3 tablespoons canola oil, plus extra for greasing tin

1 extra-large egg

⅔ cup buttermilk

1¾ cups all-purpose flour

1 teaspoon baking soda

3½ teaspoons ground ginger

½ teaspoon ground cinnamon

¼ cup firmly packed dark brown sugar

1   Put the dates in a small bowl, then pour over ½ cup of boiling water. Let cool for 30 minutes. Lightly grease an 8 inch square, 2 inch deep cake pan with canola oil, then line the bottom with parchment paper.

2   Put the butter into a small saucepan with the molasses and corn syrup. Put over low heat to melt the butter, then remove and pour in the oil. Set aside. Preheat the oven to 325°F.

3   Blend the dates and their liquid in a mini blender or small food processor to a thick puree. Beat the egg in a small bowl and stir in the buttermilk. Mix the flour with the baking soda, ginger, cinnamon, and sugar. Pour the egg, the date, and the molasses mixtures into the bowl with the flour mixture and beat briefly together with a wooden spoon just until well mixed. The mixture will be soft like a thick batter. Pour it into the lined pan, level the batter, and bake for 50–55 minutes. To test if done, insert a toothpick in the center. If it comes out clean with no uncooked batter on it, and the cake feels firm but springy to the touch, it should be done.

4   Let stand in the pan for a few minutes before removing to a wire rack, peeling off the lining paper, and letting cool completely. Wrap well and, if you desire, let stand for a day before slicing for it to become even stickier. It will keep for up to 1 week.

Let the dates provide some of the stickiness, instead of relying on all sugar and syrup. Replace milk and most of the butter with buttermilk and canola oil to lower fat and saturated fat

Banana bread

For such an easy cake to mix, this fruity loaf packs loads of flavor. With that, however, comes a lot of sugar, fat, and saturated fat. While cutting back on these, I've found ways to still keep its sweet butteriness.

	Classic	Lighter
Kcals	290	194
Fat	16.6 g	8.5 g
Sat fat	6.8 g	2 g
Sugar	17 g	11.4 g

Per slice 194 kcals

Protein 4.3 g, carbs 24.7 g, fat 8.5 g, sat fat 2 g, fiber 1.4 g, sugar 11.4g, sodium 120 mg

Cuts into 12 slices

Prep: 25 minutes
Cook: 50–55 minutes

2 very ripe medium bananas, preferably with black skins

finely grated zest of ½ lemon

½ teaspoon vanilla extract

1⅓ cups all-purpose flour

⅓ cup whole-wheat flour

1½ teaspoons baking powder

½ teaspoon baking soda

¼ cup ground almonds (almond meal)

2 tablespoons butter, at soft room temperature, cut into pieces

⅓ cup firmly packed light brown sugar

¼ cup chopped pecans or walnuts

2 large eggs

½ cup plain yogurt

3 tablespoons canola oil, plus extra for greasing

1   Preheat the oven to 350°F. Lightly grease an 8½ x 5 x 2½ inch loaf pan with canola oil, then line the bottom with parchment paper. Peel the bananas, break in pieces into a bowl, then mash them as smoothly as you can with a fork; don't worry if there are a few small lumps. Stir in the lemon zest and vanilla extract.

2   Mix both the flours with the baking powder, baking soda, and ground almonds in a large mixing bowl. Rub the butter into the flour mixture with your fingertips, then add the sugar and rub the mixture between your fingers to break down any small lumps. Stir in the nuts. Make a well in the center. Beat the eggs in a bowl, then stir in the yogurt and oil. Add this mixture along with the mashed banana to the well and briefly and gently stir together, using a large metal spoon, so that everything is just combined, without overmixing.

3   Spoon the batter into the pan and level the top. Bake for 50–55 minutes or until a toothpick inserted into the center of the cake comes out clean, laying a piece of aluminum foil over the top toward the end if it is starting to brown too quickly. Let the banana bread stand in the pan for 5 minutes, then loosen the sides with a blunt knife, turn it out onto a wire rack to finish cooling, and peel off the lining paper. Keeps moist, well wrapped, for several days.

Reduce the sugar by using dark brown for its intense, rich flavor and really ripe bananas—the blacker the better, because they get sweeter as they darken

Peanut butter cookies

Just as the name of these cookies conjures up a favorite childhood treat, it's also a giveaway to the amount of fat and sugar they may contain. By incorporating the familiar ingredients but making a few considered adjustments, this version remains faithful to the original taste and texture while offering a lighter alternative.

	Classic	Lighter
Kcals	149	106
Fat	8.8 g	6.4 g
Sat fat	3.7 g	2 g
Sugar	7.5 g	4.1 g

Per cookie 106 kcals

Protein 2.5g, carbs 9.5g, fat 6.4g, sat fat 2.0g, fiber 0.8g, sugar 4.1g, sodium 80 mg

Makes 20

Prep: 25 minutes, plus chilling
Cook: 10–12 minutes

4 tablespoon butter, at room temperature

¼ cup firmly packed light brown sugar

2 tablespoons graunlated sugar

⅓ cup plus 1 tablespoon chunky peanut butter, with no added sugar

1 tablespoon canola oil, plus 2 teaspoons

1 large egg, beaten

½ teaspoon vanilla extract

1¼ cups all-purpose flour

½ teaspoon baking powder

¼ teaspoon baking soda

3 tablespoons coarsely chopped oven-roasted, unsalted peanuts

Lower the sugar by using less and enhancing the flavor with vanilla, and choose peanut butter with no added sugar

1 Line a large baking sheet with parchment paper (or 2 if you have them). Preheat the oven to 350°F. In a large bowl, beat together the butter, both the sugars, and the peanut butter with a wooden spoon until light and well blended. Beat in all the oil, then the egg and vanilla extract. Combine the flour, baking powder, and baking soda, then stir this into the mixture, half at a time, along with the peanuts to make a soft dough. Shape the dough into a log shape, wrap it in parchment paper and chill for 30 minutes.

2 Slice the dough into 20 even pieces, then shape and roll each piece between your hands into small balls. On the work surface, flatten each one with your fingers into a 2½ inch circle, smoothing the tops and neatening the edges. Place them 1 inch apart on the lined baking sheet or sheets (bake them in batches, if necessary). Press them gently with the back of a fork to make a pattern of lines.

3 Bake for 10–12 minutes or until pale golden. Transfer to a wire rack to cool.

Chocolate cupcakes

They may be one of the prettiest baked goods around, but with the generous swirls of frosting on top and buttery sponge below, cupcakes can get incredibly high in fat, saturated fat, and sugar. All these, along with calories, have been amazingly reduced—yet these lighter cupcakes have lost none of their irresistible taste and glamour.

	Classic	Lighter
Kcals	459	234
Fat	26.1 g	10.4 g
Sat fat	16 g	4.4 g
Sugar	43.9 g	18.5 g

Per serving 234 kcals

Protein 6.7 g, carbs 27.8 g, fat 10.4 g, sat fat 4.4 g, fiber 1.3 g, sugar 18.5 g, sodium 240 mg

Makes 12

Prep: 35 minutes, plus cooling
Cook: 20 minutes

For the cakes

1⅓ cups all-purpose flour

2 tablespoons unsweetened cocoa powder, sifted

1 tablespoon baking powder

¾ cup granulated sugar

¼ cup ground almonds (almond meal)

2 extra-large eggs

¾ cup plain yogurt

2–3 drops vanilla extract

2 tablespoons butter, melted

2 tablespoons canola oil

For the frosting

1 oz bittersweet or semisweet chocolate, finely chopped, plus 1 rounded tablespoon grated chocolate for decorating

2 tablespoons butter, at soft room temperature

⅓ cup confectioners' sugar

1 tablespoon unsweetened cocoa powder

1 teaspoon low-fat milk

½ cup cold light cream cheese

½ cup quark cheese or Greek yogurt

1 Preheat the oven to 350°C. For the cakes, line a 12-section muffin pan with pretty paper muffin liners. Put the flour into a large mixing bowl, remove 2 tablespoons of it, and replace with the cocoa. Stir in the baking powder, sugar, and ground almonds, then make a well in the center. Beat the eggs in a separate bowl with a fork and stir in the yogurt and vanilla. Pour this mixture, along with the melted butter and oil, into the dry mixture and stir briefly together with a large metal spoon, just so that everything is well combined.

2 Divide the batter evenly among the paper liners. Bake for 20 minutes, until well risen. Remove and cool completely on a wire rack.

3 To make the frosting, put the chocolate into a heatproof bowl, set it over a saucepan of gently simmering water (so that the bowl does not touch the water), then remove from the heat and let stand until melted and cooled.

4 Put the butter, confectioners' sugar, cocoa, and milk in a medium bowl, then beat with a wooden spoon until smooth. Next, beat in the cream cheese and quark. When the chocolate has cooled, stir it into the cream cheese mixture. Spoon, then spread the frosting in big swirls over each cupcake and sprinkle with the grated chocolate. They will keep for up to 2–3 days in the refrigerator.

Reduce fat as well as sugar by using light cream cheese and quark to give the frosting its creamy bulk, instead of using all butter and confectioners' sugar

Blueberry muffins

These are light, fluffy muffins with added fruit and taste. Adding bananas and lemon will boost the flavor and eliminate the need for salt.

	Classic	Lighter
Kcals	234	206
Fat	9 g	6 g
Sat fat	5 g	1 g
Sugar	16.4 g	16 g

Per muffin 206 kcals

Protein 5 g, carbs 36 g, fat 6 g, sat fat 1 g, fiber 2 g, sugar 16 g, sodium 172 mg

Makes 12

Prep: 25 minutes
Cook: 20–25 minutes

⅓ cup canola oil

1¾ cups all-purpose flour

¾ cup whole-wheat flour

3¾ teaspoons baking powder

finely grated zest of ½ lemon, plus 1 teaspoon lemon juice

⅓ cup granulated sugar

¼ cup firmly packed light brown sugar

1 small ripe banana with black skin

1 extra-large egg

1¼ cups buttermilk

1½ cups fresh blueberries

1 Preheat the oven to 400°F. Use 1 teaspoon of the oil to lightly grease a 12-section muffin pan (or use paper liners).

2 Mix both flours with the baking powder and lemon zest. Reserve 1 tablespoon of the granulated sugar, then stir the rest into the flour with the brown sugar.

3 Mash the banana well. In another bowl, beat the egg, then stir in the banana, buttermilk, and remaining oil. Using a large metal spoon, lightly stir into the flour mixture, just to combine; overmixing will make the muffins tough. Toss in the blueberries and give just a few turns of the spoon to carefully stir them in without crushing.

4 Spoon the batter into the pan, with each section of the pan or liner being full. Bake for 20–25 minutes, until risen and golden.

5 Mix the reserved granulated sugar with the lemon juice. When the muffins are done, remove from the oven, then brush with the sugar and lemon mixture while they are still hot. Gently loosen the edges of each muffin with a blunt knife, then keep them in the pan for 15 minutes to cool a little because they are delicate while hot. Remove to a wire rack. These are best eaten the day they are made.

use buttermilk instead of milk to lower fat and saturated fat

Chocolate chip cookies

The size of American cookies seems to get larger and larger, but make them too small and we feel cheated. These cookies are the perfect balancing act of size and ingredients.

	Classic	Lighter
Kcals	162	97
Fat	10 g	5 g
Sat fat	6 g	3 g
Sugar	11 g	6 g

Per cookie 97 kcals

Protein 1 g, carbs 12 g, fat 5 g, sat fat 3 g, fiber 1 g, sugar 6 g, sodium 48 mg

Makes 22

Prep: 25 minutes, plus cooling
and standing
Cook: 12 minutes per batch

6 tablespoons butter

1 tablespoon unsweetened
cocoa powder

1 teaspoon instant coffee granules

⅓ cup firmly packed light brown sugar

2 tablespoons granulated sugar

3 oz bittersweet chocolate

1 large egg, beaten

½ teaspoon vanilla extract

1¼ cups all-purpose flour

½ teaspoon baking soda

1 Line a couple of baking sheets with parchment paper. Put the butter, cocoa, and coffee into a medium saucepan, then heat gently until the butter has melted. Remove from the heat, stir in both the sugars, then let cool.

2 Chop the chocolate into small pieces. Beat the egg and vanilla into the cooled butter mixture to make a smooth mixture. Stir the flour and baking soda together. Add to the butter mixture with two-thirds of the chocolate, then gently stir together to combine. Don't overmix. Let stand for 10–15 minutes until slightly firm, ready for shaping.

3 Preheat the oven to 350°F. Using your hands, shape the dough into 22 small balls. Lay them on the lined sheets, spaced well apart so that they have room to spread (you may have to bake in batches). Press the rest of the chocolate pieces on top of each cookie. (They can be frozen on the sheets and then transferred to bags at this stage, and kept in the freezer for up to 1 month.) Bake for 12 minutes. Let stand on the sheets for a couple of minutes, then transfer to a wire rack to cool.

Add less sugar, but intensify
the flavor and moistness by
using granulated mixed with
light brown

Raspberry sponge cake

Simply reducing the ingredients won't work with this classic recipe, so I've worked out some alternatives that will still provide the cake's characteristic texture and taste. Now you CAN have your cake and eat it.

	Classic	Lighter
Kcals	371	263
Fat	20.3 g	9.3 g
Sat fat	12 g	2.8 g
Sugar	27.4 g	24.1 g

Per slice 263 kcals

Protein 5.6 g, carbs 39 g, fat 9.3 g, sat fat 2.8 g, fiber 1.3 g, sugar 24.1 g, sodium 240 mg

Cuts into 8 slices

Prep: 25 minutes
Cook: 20 minutes

1⅓ cups all-purpose flour

1 tablespoon baking powder

¾ cup granulated sugar

¼ cup ground almonds (almond meal)

2 extra-large eggs

¾ cup plain yogurt

2–3 drops vanilla extract

2 tablespoons butter, melted

2 tablespoons canola oil, plus extra for greasing

¼ cup raspberry preserves

½ teaspoon confectioners' sugar, to decorate

1 Preheat the oven to 350°F. Lightly grease two 7 inch cake pans (preferably loose-bottom) with canola oil, then line the bottoms with parchment paper. Put the flour, baking powder, granulated sugar, and ground almonds into a large mixing bowl, then make a well in the center. Beat the eggs in a separate bowl, then stir in the yogurt and vanilla. Pour this mixture, along with the melted butter and oil, into the dry mixture and stir briefly together with a large metal spoon until well combined.

2 Divide the batter evenly between the 2 pans and level the tops. Bake both cakes, side by side, for 20 minutes, until risen and beginning to come away slightly from the edges of the pans.

3 Remove the cakes from the oven and loosen the sides with a blunt knife. Let the cakes cool briefly in the pans, then turn them out. If the pans have a loose bottom, an easy way is to sit the pan on an upturned jar and let the outer ring of the pan drop down. Peel off the lining paper and sit the cakes on a wire rack. Let stand until completely cold.

4 Put one of the cakes on a serving plate and spread over the preserves. Put the other cake on top and sift over the confectioners' sugar, or make a pattern using a paper template.

Greatly reduce the butter and replace with yogurt and canola oil as substitutes to cut the fat farther, especially saturated fat

Oatmeal bars

Oatmeal bars hold together in such a mouth-watering way, but that is due to all the butter and sugar required to make the oats stick. The trick in this healthier version is to stir in some grated apple so that less butter and sugar are needed—but each bar remains sticky, chewy, and delicious.

	Classic	Lighter
Kcals	215	157
Fat	11.5 g	8.4 g
Sat fat	6.7 g	2.9 g
Sugar	13.1 g	8.3 g

Per oatmeal bar 157 kcals

Protein 3 g, carbs 16.1 g, fat 8.4 g, sat fat 2.9 g, fiber 2.1 g, sugar 8.3 g, sodium 40 mg

Makes 18

Prep: 20 minutes
Cook: 30–35 minutes

6 tablespoons butter, cut into pieces

¼ cup demerara or other raw sugar

2 tablespoons packed dark brown sugar

3 tablespoons light corn syrup

3 tablespoons canola oil

2¾ cups rolled oats

¼ cup finely chopped toasted hazelnuts

1 large Pippin or other sweet, crisp apple, peeled and cored

2 tablespoons sunflower seeds

1 tablespoon golden flaxseed

1 Preheat the oven to 350°F. Line the bottom of a 11 x 7 inch shallow baking pan with parchment paper (no need to grease). Put the butter, both sugars, and the corn syrup in a medium saucepan over medium heat. Heat until the butter has melted, stirring occasionally. The sugar doesn't need to completely dissolve. Remove from the heat and stir in the oil, oats, and hazelnuts. Grate the apple on the coarsest side of your grater and stir into the mixture.

2 Transfer the oat mixture to the lined pan and spread it out evenly. Sprinkle with the sunflower seeds and flaxseed and pat them firmly into the surface.

3 Bake for 25–30 minutes or until set and golden brown. Loosen from the sides of the pan so that it doesn't stick. Mark into 18 bars with a sharp knife, then let cool before cutting through the markings again and lifting the bars out of the pan.

Reduce fat and sugar by mixing in some grated apple to create stickiness and increase fiber

Oat and raisin cookies

Getting the perfect balance of crispness and chewiness for most classic cookies is usually determined by the amount of fat and sugar you need to add. To find ways to get them both to a healthier minimum, I've made careful ingredient and baking choices to make sure that these cookies are still great for munching on.

	Classic	Lighter
Kcals	218	116
Fat	11 g	5.6 g
Sat fat	5.3 g	2 g
Sugar	15.1 g	8.2 g

Per cookie 116 kcals

Protein 1.8 g, carbs 14.2 g, fat 5.6 g, sat fat 2 g, fiber 1 g, sugar 8.2 g, sodium 40 mg

Makes 15

Prep: 25 minutes, plus cooling
Cook: 10 minutes per batch

4 tablespoons butter

3 tablespoons canola oil

1 tablespoon light corn syrup

⅓ cup whole-wheat flour

⅓ cup all-purpose flour

½ cup plus 1 tablespoon rolled oats

¼ cup firmly packed light brown sugar

¼ teaspoon baking powder

¼ teaspoon baking soda

½ teaspoon ground cinnamon

½ cup raisins

1 large egg, beaten

1 Preheat the oven to 350°F. Line a large baking sheet (or 2 if you have them) with parchment paper.

2 Melt the butter in a small saucepan, then remove from the heat and spoon in the oil and corn syrup. Set aside to cool slightly. Mix both the flours and the oats in a large mixing bowl with the sugar, baking powder, baking soda, cinnamon, and raisins. Make a well in the center of the flour mixture, pour in the butter and oil, then add the egg. Stir all together to mix to a soft, slightly sticky dough.

3 Divide, then shape the dough into 15 smooth, even balls. Place them on the baking sheet, spaced well apart to allow room for the dough to spread, then flatten with your fingers to about 2½ inch circles. Bake for about 10 minutes (in batches) or until golden. Let cool on the baking sheet for a couple of minutes, then transfer to a wire rack to finish cooling.

Line your baking sheet with parchment paper so that you don't need extra butter for greasing

Almond tart

This is my spin on a British classic tart. The trick is to replace half the almonds with cornmeal to cut down on the fat while maintaining the tart's characteristic texture. The tart is even softer when eaten the next day.

	Classic	Lighter
Kcals	429	280
Fat	28.2 g	16.2 g
Sat fat	12.5 g	3.9 g
Sugar	20.3 g	12.8 g

Per serving 280 kcals

Protein 5.9 g, carbs 27.2 g, fat 16.2 g, sat fat 3.9 g, fiber 1.1 g, sugar 12.8 g, sodium 160 mg

Serves 8

Prep: 25 minutes
Cook: 50 minutes

1 sheet store-bought rolled dough pie crust, thawed if frozen

all-purpose flour, for dusting

¾ cup fresh raspberries

1 tablespoon raspberry preserves or jam

1 tablespoon slivered almonds

1 heaping tablespoon confectioners' sugar, sifted

For the filling

½ cup ground almonds (almond meal)

⅓ cup cornmeal

¼ cup granulated sugar, plus 2 teaspoons

½ teaspoon baking powder

2 large eggs

½ cup plain yogurt

scant ½ teaspoon almond extract

2 tablespoons canola oil

1 Preheat the oven to 400°F. Thinly roll out the dough on a lightly floured surface. Line an 8 inch fluted tart pan with the dough, easing the dough into the pan carefully to prevent it from stretching. Run a rolling pin over the top of the pan to trim off any excess dough. Prick the dough bottom lightly with a fork. Put the pan on a baking sheet. Line the dough with aluminum foil and pie weights or dried beans and bake for 12 minutes, until the pastry is set.

2 Meanwhile, to start the filling, heat a small, dry nonstick pan, add the ground almonds and gently heat, stirring often, for 2–3 minutes to lightly brown. Transfer to a mixing bowl to cool.

3 Remove the foil and weights from the pastry shell and bake for another 5 minutes, until pale golden. Remove and reduce the oven to 350°F.

4 Using a fork, mash the raspberries in a small bowl with the preserves or jam. Spread it in pastry shell over its bottom. Put the cornmeal, sugar, and baking powder in the bowl with the ground almonds and stir to combine. Make a well in the center. Beat the eggs in a separate bowl, then beat in the yogurt and almond extract. Add this, along with the oil, to the dry ingredients and gently stir together with a large metal spoon so that everything is just combined; don't overmix.

5 Pour the almond filling over the raspberry mixture and sprinkle the slivered almonds over the top. Bake for 30 minutes or until the top is risen and pale golden. Cool slightly, then remove from the pan.

6 Mix the confectioners' sugar with a few drops of cold water to make a thickish icing, then use a teaspoon to drizzle it over the cooled tart.

use polenta to replace some of the ground almonds, then enhance the flavor with almond extract

Chocolate log

Though traditionally served at Christmas, this lighter chocolate log, made without butter and cream, can be a year-round favorite. With a few cake-making and ingredient changes, it remains rich and elegant.

	Classic	Lighter
Kcals	482	271
Fat	29 g	13 g
Sat fat	16 g	7 g
Sugar	42 g	22 g

Per serving 271 kcals

Protein 8 g, carbs 33 g, fat 13 g, sat fat 7 g, fiber 1 g, sugar 22 g, sodium 116 mg

Serves 10

Prep: 35 minutes, plus cooling
Cook: 12–15 minutes

For the sponge

canola oil, for greasing

1 teaspoon instant coffee granules

4 extra-large eggs, at room temperature

⅓ cup granulated sugar, plus extra for rolling

¼ cup lgihtly packed light brown sugar

1 cup all-purpose flour

1 teaspoon baking powder

2 tablespoons unsweetened cocoa powder

For the frosting

2 oz bittersweet chocolate, finely chopped

1 cuplight mascarpone cheese

⅔ cup quark cheese or Greek yogurt

⅓ cup confectioners' sugar

1½ tablespoons unsweetened cocoa powder

1 teaspoon instant coffee granules

½ teaspoon vanilla extract

holly sprigs, to decorate (optional)

1 Preheat the oven to 375°F. Lightly grease a 9 x 13 inch jellyroll pan with canola oil, then line with parchment paper.

2 Mix the coffee for the sponge with 1 tablespoon of warm water. Beat together the eggs, both sugars, and the coffee mixture in a large mixing bowl with an electric mixer for about 8 minutes or until the mixture is thick and airy like meringue and holds a trail when you lift up the beaters.

3 Sift the flour, baking powder, and cocoa powder over the fluffy egg mixture, then fold in gently, using a large metal spoon. Pour the batter evenly into the lined pan and carefully tip it so that it spreads evenly without being deflated. Use a knife, if necessary, to gently tease it into the corners. Bake for 12–15 minutes or until the cake feels spongy but firm when touched.

4 Lay a sheet of parchment paper on the work surface and sprinkle with a little granulated sugar. Turn the pan upside down onto the paper and let the cake fall out. Carefully peel off the paper. Roll up the cake lengthwise from one of the short ends with the help of the paper, rolling it inside so that the cake doesn't stick. Cool. (The cake becomes even more moist if left overnight wrapped up, then frosting the next day.)

5 For the chocolate frosting, put the chopped chocolate in a medium heatproof bowl. Heat a small saucepan of water (one-third full) until boiling, remove it from the heat, then sit the bowl of chocolate over the top. Let stand for a few minutes off the heat until melted. Remove the bowl from the pan, then let the chocolate stand until it is cool to the touch.

6 Beat the mascarpone and quark together in a mixing bowl, then sift and stir in the confectioners' sugar and cocoa powder. Stir in the cooled melted chocolate (reserving a couple of teaspoons for drizzling), then the coffee mixed with the vanilla extract.

7 Carefully unroll the cake—don't worry if it cracks a little—and discard the lining paper. Spread half of the frosting over the unrolled cake, then reroll it, finishing with the seam underneath. Place the cake on a serving plate. Swirl the rest of the frosting all over the cake to cover it, then drizzle with the reserved melted chocolate. Decorate with sprigs of holly, if you desire.

Replace butter and cream for the frosting and filling with light mascarpone and quark to reduce fat

•

Use less chocolate and bump up the taste with cocoa, coffee, and vanilla extract

•

Make an frosting that requires less sugar

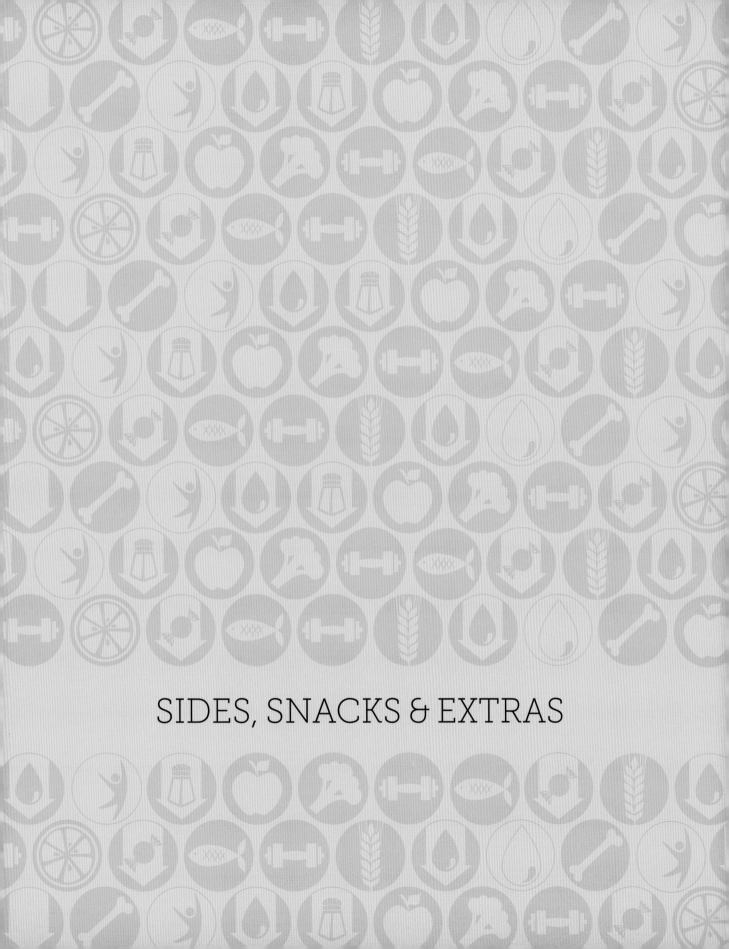

SIDES, SNACKS & EXTRAS

The big breakfast

Have you ever tucked into a big breakfast, then felt racked with guilt? This is a more contemporary British-style version, using sausages with the highest meat content, and as little fat and sodium as possible.

	Classic	Lighter
Kcals	807	618
Fat	63 g	37 g
Sat fat	18 g	11 g
Sodium	1,808 mg	1,220 mg

Per serving 618 kcals

Protein 37 g, carbs 37 g, fat 37 g, sat fat 11 g, fiber 5 g, sugar 21 g, sodium 1,220 mg

Serves 2

Prep: 5 minutes
Cook: about 20 minutes

4 good-quality lean unsmoked bacon slices

4 portobello mushrooms, trimmed

12–16 cherry tomatoes on the vine, at room temperature

2 tablespoons olive oil

2 slices multigrain or whole-grain bread, cut on the diagonal

2 good-quality pork sausages, minimum 86% pork

2 extra-large eggs, at room temperature

few drops cider vinegar

1 cup freshly squeezed orange juice

1 orange, cut into wedges

⅓ cup fresh blueberries

1 Lay the bacon, mushrooms, and tomatoes on an aluminum foil-lined baking sheet. Brush the tops of the mushrooms with 1 tablespoon of the oil and both sides of the bread with the remaining oil. Set aside.

2 Preheat the broiler to high. Lay the sausages on a small aluminum foil-lined baking sheet (best not to prick good-quality sausages or they may lose moisture). Broil for about 10 minutes, until cooked, turning occasionally.

3 Meanwhile, fill three-quarters of a small saucepan and a wide, deep sauté pan with water. Bring both to a boil. Lower one whole egg into the small saucepan and remove after 30 seconds. Crack the egg into a cup. Add vinegar to the larger pan, then, using a wire whisk, swirl the water around to create a whirlpool. Remove the whisk and slowly add the egg into the center of the whirlpool. When the water comes back to a boil, remove the pan from the heat, cover, and let stand for 3 minutes, then remove the egg. Place in a bowl of warm water while you cook the other egg. Alternatively, cook both eggs an hour ahead, let stand in a bowl of iced water, then reheat for 1½ minutes in simmering water before serving.

4 While the eggs are cooking, heat a ridged grill pan to hot. Place the bacon, tomatoes, mushrooms ,and tomatoes under the broiler for 3–4 minutes without turning. At the same time, lay the bread on the grill pan and cook for about 1 minute each side until crisp. Drain everything on paper towels.

5 Remove the eggs with a slotted spoon and drain briefly on paper towels. Arrange everything on a plate and serve with the juice and fruit.

choose ingredients wisely by checking and comparing amounts on the labels of bread, bacon, and sausages to reduce sodium

Crunchy granola

Many granolas are overly sweet, and with all the seeds, nuts, and oil to make them crunchy, are in danger of being too high in fat. This one still packs a good crunch and will keep you going all through the morning.

	Classic	Lighter
Kcals	283	236
Fat	17.6 g	13.2 g
Sat fat	2.1 g	1.5 g
Sugar	7.6 g	4.4 g

Per serving 236 kcals

Protein 7.1 g, carbs 19.5 g, fat 13.2 g, sat fat 1.5 g, fiber 4.5 g, sugar 4.4 g, sodium 0 mg

Makes 18 servings (about ⅓ cup)

Prep: 15 minutes
Cook: 20–25 minutes

5 cups rolled oats

¼ cup sliced or chopped almonds, in skins

½ cup chopped pecans

½ cup coarsely chopped hazelnuts, in skins

⅓ cup sunflower seeds

¼ cup pumpkin seeds

¼ cup golden flaxseed

3 tablespoons sesame seeds

¼ cup canola oil

2 tablespoons honey

2 teaspoons black molasses

⅓ cup dried blueberries or cranberries

1 Preheat the oven to 375°F. Line a large baking sheet with parchment paper. Put the oats into a large bowl, then stir in all the nuts and seeds.

2 Measure the canola oil into a small bowl and stir in the honey and black molassses. Pour this into the bowl of oats and give it all a good stir so that everything is evenly coated and to break up any clumps of oats that form. I find a large fork does this job best.

3 Spread the mixture onto the baking sheet. The mixture needs to spread out so that it can brown in the oven. Bake for 20–25 minutes, forking through 2–3 times so that the parts underneath that aren't getting brown can come to the surface. When golden all through, remove from the oven and stir in the dried blueberries or cranberries. Let cool and become crunchy, then pack into an airtight container to store.

TIPS

- If you first measure the oil in the measuring spoon, then pour the honey into it afterward without washing it, the honey just slides out.
- Stir the dried fruit in after baking instead of beforehand, otherwise cooking hardens it.

Use a little black molasses to help sweeten. Its concentrated taste means you need less honey or added sugar

Spanish omelet

Traditionally, the sliced potatoes and onions for a Spanish omelet are stewed in a copious amount of oil before being stirred into the eggs. To lighten up the recipe, I've cooked them in the oven instead.

	Classic	Lighter
Kcals	558	295
Fat	38.9 g	16.5 g
Sat fat	6.7 g	3.5 g
Sodium	240 mg	200 mg

Per serving 295 kcals

Protein 12.1 g, carbs 24.2 g, fat 16.5 g, sat fat 3.5 g, fiber 4.2 g, sugar 6.3 g, sodium 200 mg

Serves 4

Prep: 25 minutes
Cook: 35 minutes

1 medium onion, thinly sliced

1 red bell pepper, cored, seeded, and thinly sliced

3 tablespoons extra virgin olive oil

1 lb 2 oz new potatoes, unpeeled and thinly sliced

4 cups spinach leaves

6 large eggs

¼ cup chopped flat leaf parsley

salt and freshly ground black pepper

1 Preheat the oven to 375°F. Sprinkle the onion on one half of a small, nonstick baking sheet and the bell pepper slices on the other half. Drizzle 1 teaspoon of the oil over the onion slices and another teaspoon over the bell pepper slices. Gently toss to coat, keeping them separate, and spread out. Spread the potatoes over a large, nonstick baking sheet and drizzle with 1 tablespoon of the oil. Toss together and season all the vegetables with black pepper. Roast for 20–25 minutes, until softened and tender but not too brown.

2 Put the spinach in a heatproof bowl and pour over enough almost boiling water to let it wilt. Let stand for 30 seconds, stir, then put it into a colander and cool under cold running water. Squeeze out all the liquid, then finely chop.

3 Beat the eggs with a fork in a large mixing bowl and pour in the cold water. Add the onion, potatoes, bell pepper, spinach, and 3 tablespoons of the parsley, and season with more black pepper and a little salt. Let the mixture stand for about 5 minutes to combine the flavors.

4 Pour 1 tablespoon of the oil into a 9–10 inch nonstick skillet and heat over medium heat. Stir the egg mixture, pour it into the pan, and spread it out evenly. As it starts to set, tilt the pan to pour some of the runny egg to the edges. After 6–7 minutes, when the edges are cooked, the underneath is slightly browned, and the inside not quite cooked, check that the omelet is not sticking on the bottom, then carefully turn it out onto a large plate.

5 Pour the remaining 1 teaspoon oil into the pan, then slide the omelet and any runny egg back in. Tuck the edges under to shape the omelet like a plump cushion and cook for about another 4 minutes, until just set. Remove and let it stand and settle for 3–4 minutes before serving. Serve hot, warm, or cold, sprinkled with the remaining parsley.

Lower the fat by roasting the vegetables in the oven with minimum oil, then cooking the omelet in a nonstick pan

Roasted vegetables

Roasted vegetables can always tempt with their golden crispiness, but this requires generous amounts of oil for cooking. In this recipe, oil is kept to a minimum by cooking the vegetables the French way, en papillote, snugly wrapped in parchment paper, so that all the flavor is trapped inside as they roast, yet they still turn deliciously golden and crisp.

	Classic	Lighter
Kcals	198	141
Fat	8.9 g	3.8 g
Sat fat	1.3 g	0.4 g
Sodium	120 mg	80 mg

Per serving 141 kcals

Protein 4 g, carbs 22.2 g, fat 3.8 g, sat fat 0.4 g, fiber 3.7 g, sugar 5.4 g, sodium 80 mg

Serves 4

Prep: 15 minutes
Cook: 30 minutes

1 red bell pepper

1 medium zucchini

14 oz new potatoes, unpeeled, scrubbed and halved

4 small shallots, halved

8 garlic cloves, peeled

4 sprigs of rosemary

4 teaspoons canola oil

salt and freshly ground black pepper

1 Preheat the oven to 400°F. Cut out four 15 inch squares of parchment paper.

2 Quarter and remove the core and seeds from the bell pepper, then cut each quarter into 4 to give you 16 pieces. Cut the zucchini into 12 thick slices.

3 Lay one quarter of all the vegetables in the center of each paper square along with 2 garlic cloves and a sprig of rosemary. Drizzle 1 teaspoon of the oil over each one. Season with black pepper and a pinch of salt. Fold the edges of the paper over to make a well-sealed package.

4 Place the packages on a large baking sheet and roast for 30 minutes, until the vegetables are tender and golden.

TIPS

- Cut the vegetables into similar-size pieces, so that they will all cook evenly together.

- This mixture of roasted vegetables makes a good accompaniment to roasted chicken or fish.

Halve the fat by roasting in paper packages and keep saturated fat to a minimum with canola oil

Hummus

One thing people love about hummus is its soft creamy texture, which comes from blending chickpeas until smooth with tahini and olive oil. By mixing in yogurt and roasted garlic, I discovered it's not necessary to use as much tahini and oil, because this lighter recipe still tastes surprisingly rich and creamy, and fat and saturated fat are more than halved.

	Classic	Lighter
Kcals	233	145
Fat	18.9 g	8.2 g
Sat fat	2.6 g	1 g
Sodium	160 mg	200 mg

Per serving 145 kcals

Protein 6.8 g, carbs 11.4 g, fat 8.2 g, sat fat 1 g, fiber 4.5 g, sugar 1.1 g, sodium 200 mg

Serves 4

Prep: 15 minutes
Cook: 25–30 minutes

1 whole garlic bulb

1 teaspoon cumin seeds

1 (15 oz) can chickpeas

2 tablespoons lemon juice, plus extra to taste (optional)

1½ tablespoons tahini

1 tablespoon canola oil

2 tablespoons plain yogurt

salt

pinch of paprika and chopped flat leaf parsley, to garnish

1 Preheat the oven to 375°F. Slice the stem end from the garlic to slightly expose the tops of the cloves. Sit the bulb in a small baking pan, then roast for 25–30 minutes, until the cloves feel soft.

2 Meanwhile, heat a small, heavy saucepan, add the cumin seeds, and heat for about a minute or until they start to smell fragrant and darken slightly in color, moving them around in the pan so that they don't burn. Grind them finely using a mortar and pestle.

3 Drain the chickpeas in a strainer over a bowl. Put the chickpeas into a blender or food processor with the lemon juice and 3 tablespoons cold water. When the garlic is softened, remove, and when cool enough to handle, separate the cloves from the bulb, squeeze out the soft flesh, and put it in with the chickpeas. Process until smooth, then spoon in the tahini, 1 teaspoon of the oil, the yogurt, ½ teaspoon of the toasted cumin, and a pinch of salt. Pulse again until soft and creamy.

4 Taste to see if you would like more lemon juice. Also, if you prefer an even softer texture, add a drop more water. Spoon and spread the hummus onto 1 large or 2 small plates, using the back of a spoon to give it a swirl. Sprinkle with a pinch of paprika, chopped parsley, and as much of the remaining cumin as you desire, then finish with a drizzle of the remaining oil.

Reduce fat by replacing some of the oil and tahini with yogurt, water, and roasted garlic to maintain flavor and creaminess

Sausage rolls

You can send the calories packing with this healthier version of a picnic favorite. It is not always clear what goes into cheaper sausagemeats, so here I've used lean ground pork, which is lower in fat.

	Classic	Lighter
Kcals	178	99
Fat	13.8 g	5.5 g
Sat fat	5 g	2 g
Sodium	332 mg	108 mg

Per sausage roll 99 kcals

Protein 5.9 g, carbs 6.8 g, fat 5.5 g, sat fat 2 g, fiber 0.6 g, sugar 0.3 g, sodium 108 mg

Makes 16

Prep: 25 minutes, plus cooling and optional chilling
Cook: 20 minutes

For the filling

1 teaspoon canola oil

1 plump shallot, finely chopped

½ cup canned or cooked green lentils

11 oz 8% fat ground pork

1 cup fresh white bread crumbs

2 teaspoons finely chopped tarragon

good pinch of dry English mustard

good pinch of grated nutmeg

all-purpose flour, for dusting

For the pastry

½ sheet ready-to-bake puff pastry

2 teaspoons low-fat milk, to glaze

salt and freshly ground black pepper

1 Preheat the oven to 425°F. Line a baking sheet with parchment paper.

2 Heat the oil in a small, nonstick skillet. Add the shallot and sauté for a few minutes, until softened. Let cool. Meanwhile, mash the lentils in a bowl with the back of a spoon, then stir in the rest of the filling ingredients, the shallot, a small pinch of salt, and a good grating of black pepper. Cover and chill for 20 minutes (not essential but makes it easier to shape).

3 Halve the filling. Lightly flour the work surface and, using your hands, roll each half, one at a time, into an 11 inch long log shape—dust more flour on the work surface if it starts to stick. Set aside.

4 Roll out the pastry on a lightly floured work surface to an 11 inch square. Cut in half to make 2 rectangles. Lay one of the log shapes along one of the long edges of one pastry rectangle. Roll the pastry around it to almost enclose, then brush a little milk down the opposite long side. Roll the seam underneath and press down to seal. Trim off the ends to neaten, if necessary, then slice into 8 rolls. Place on a baking sheet, with the seams underneath. Using the blunt side of the knife, make 3 indents on top of each roll. Repeat with the rest of the pastry and filling. Brush the tops with a little milk.

5 Bake for 18–20 minutes, until golden and slightly puffy. Remove from the sheet and cool on a wire rack. Serve warm or cold.

use lean pork mince instead of sausagemeat to reduce the fat. substitute some of the meat with green lentils to reduce saturated fat

Beef turnovers

Don't miss out on a lunchtime convenience food. The key to this healthier recipe is in the pastry—how it's made, decreasing the size of the turnover and reducing the thickness of the crust.

	Classic	Lighter
Kcals	821	511
Fat	50.6 g	25.2 g
Sat fat	27.8 g	10.7 g
Sodium	760 mg	320 mg

Per pasty 511 kcals

Protein 22.1 g, carbs 48.5 g, fat 25.2 g, sat fat 10.7 g, fiber 2.8 g, sugar 3.1 g, sodium 320 g

Makes 6

Prep: 1 hour
Cook: 50 minutes

For the filling

14 oz skirt steak, trimmed of excess fat, cut into small chunks

1 cup diced potato

1 cup diced rutabaga

1 medium onion, finely chopped

3 tablespoons chopped parsley

1 tablespoon Worcestershire sauce

For the pastry dough

2¾ cups all-purpose flour, plus extra for dusting

1¼ teaspoons baking powder

6 tablespoons cold butter, cut into small pieces

3 tablespoons extra virgin canola oil

1 extra-large egg, separated

salt and freshly ground black pepper

1 Preheat the oven to 400°F. Line 1–2 baking sheets with parchment paper.

2 To make the filling, mix everything together in a bowl with ¾ teaspoon black pepper and 1 tablespoon cold water. Stir in a pinch of salt and set aside.

3 To make the pastry, put the flour, baking powder, and butter in a food processor. Pulse until the mixture resembles fine bread crumbs. Add the oil, egg yolk, and ⅓ cup of cold water. Pulse again until the dough just starts to come together, adding another ½–1 tablespoon water, or as needed. If you gently press the dough and it sticks together, you know that it's the right consistency. Turn out the dough onto the work surface and gently press it into a smooth ball.

4 Cut the dough into 6 equal pieces. For each turnover, lightly and briefly shape one piece of the dough into a smooth ball. (Keep the other pieces wrapped in plastic wrap until needed.) Press the ball down to make an even flattened circle. Then roll the dough out on a lightly floured surface, as thinly as you can, to a circle just over 8 inches in diameter. Because you are rolling the dough thinner than usual, handle it carefully to prevent it from breaking, and keep the work surface and rolling pin lightly dusted with flour to prevent the dough from sticking. Use the bottom of an 8 inch loose-bottom cake pan (or similar) as a guide to cut around to neaten the dough edges.

5 Spoon a sixth of the filling down the center of the dough circle and lightly press down with your hand to contain and flatten it slightly. Dampen the dough edges with water and carefully bring one side of the dough over to join the other side, tucking in the filling to keep it inside as you do so. Press the seam together to seal, then make a thin decorative edge by rolling or curling the dough edge over all the way around. Press down to seal. Repeat with the remaining dough and filling.

6 Sit each turnover on the lined baking sheet(s), then pierce a small hole in the top of each one for the steam to escape. Beat the egg white to loosen, then brush a little over each turnover to glaze.

7 Bake for 15 minutes, then reduce the oven temperature to 350°F. Brush with more egg white and bake for another 35 minutes, until the turnover is crisp and golden, covering loosely with aluminum foil if they are browning too quickly. Remove with a wide spatula and let cool slightly on a wire rack. Serve warm or cold.

Lower fat by trimming any excess from the meat

•

Use less fat in the dough, replacing some of the butter with canola oil to reduce the level of saturated fat

•

Roll the dough out thinner so that less is required

•

Season the filling generously with black pepper so that less salt is needed

Garlic bread

Oozing with butter as you take the first mouthful, garlic bread is a treat that can set your heart pounding just thinking of it. With a few sneaky changes, this recipe has half the saturated fat of the classic, but its rich garlicky taste still soaks deeply into each slice of bread.

	Classic	Lighter
Kcals	230	160
Fat	11.4 g	8.3 g
Sat fat	6.7 g	3.1 g
Sodium	320 mg	240 mg

Per serving (2 slices) 160 kcals

Protein 4.8 g, carbs 16.6 g, fat 8.3 g, sat fat 3.1 g, fiber 1.3 g, sugar 1.1 g, sodium 240 mg

Serves 8 (2 slices per serving)

Prep: 20 minutes
Cook: 12 minutes

2 tablespoon unsalted butter, at room temperature

2 tablespoons mayonnaise

½ cup grated mozzarella cheese

2 teaspoons extra virgin olive oil

3 garlic cloves, crushed

1 tablespoon finely chopped parsley

1 tablespoon snipped chives

1 (9½ oz) ciabatta loaf

freshly ground black pepper

1 Preheat the oven to 375°F. Beat the butter and mayonnaise together in a bowl until well blended and smooth. Mix in the mozzarella, oil, and garlic, then stir in the parsley and chives. Season with a little black pepper.

2 Slice the ciabatta in half horizontally. Spread the garlic mixture over the cut sides of each half. Wrap each half loosely in aluminum foil. Place both packages on a large baking sheet and bake for 10 minutes. Remove.

3 Preheat the broiler to high. Open up the packages and broil for about 2 minutes or until bubbling, crisp and golden. Slice each piece into 8 to serve.

Halve the saturated fat by replacing most of the butter with a mixture of mozzarella cheese, mayonnaise, and olive oil

Braised leeks and peas

It's low in fat, counts as one of your five a day, is good for you and packed full of flavors. Serve this as a side dish with salmon or chicken.

	Classic	Lighter
Kcals	90	56
Fat	4.1 g	1.9 g
Sat fat	2.3 g	0.3 g
Sodium	80 mg	160 mg

Per serving 56 kcals

Protein 3.6 g, carbs 6.1 g, fat 1.9 g, sat fat 0.3 g, fiber 3.5 g, sugar 2.5 g, sodium 160 g

Serves 6

Prep: 5 minutes
Cook: 20 minutes

6 leeks, trimmed

1 cup chicken or vegetable stock

3 garlic cloves, sliced

4 sprigs of thyme, plus extra leaves to serve

1⅓ cups frozen peas

2 teaspoons olive oil

freshly ground black pepper

1 Discard the outer, darker, tougher leaves from the leeks, then halve each into 2 shorter lengths and rinse under cold running water.

2 Pour the chicken or vegetable stock into a large, wide shallow saucepan, then sprinkle in the garlic and sprigs of thyme. Lay the leeks in the pan, trying not to crowd them, then season with black pepper. Cover and simmer for 15 minutes, until almost tender.

3 Add the peas to the pan, bring back to a boil, and simmer for another 5 minutes, until the vegetables are cooked.

4 Using a slotted spoon, transfer the leeks, peas, and garlic to a warm serving dish, season with extra black pepper, drizzle with the olive oil, and finish with a sprinkling of thyme leaves.

Replace butter with olive oil to lower saturated fat, and create extra flavor with garlic and thyme

Ratatouille

By roasting the eggplants with the other vegetables instead of frying them, the fat is kept to a minimum. To enhance the flavor, I've borrowed food writer Elizabeth David's idea of adding crushed coriander seeds.

	Classic	Lighter
Kcals	249	161
Fat	18.2 g	8.8 g
Sat fat	2.8 g	1.4 g
Sodium	360 mg	80 mg

Per serving 161 kcals

Protein 5.1 g, carbs 15.6 g, fat 8.8 g, sat fat 1.4 g, fiber 7.5 g, sugar 13.7 g, sodium 80 mg

Serves 4

Prep: 35 minutes
Cook: 45 minutes

2 red bell peppers, cored, seeded, and cut into 1 inch pieces

2 medium zucchini, cut into 1 inch pieces

1 large eggplant, cut into 1 inch pieces

2 tablespoons olive oil, plus 2 teaspoons

2 sprigs of thyme

2 sprigs of rosemary

1 bay leaf

1 onion, chopped

4 garlic cloves, finely chopped

4 tomatoes

1 teaspoon coriander seeds, crushed

salt and freshly ground black pepper

handful of chopped fresh cilantro and flat leaf parsley, to garnish

1 Preheat the oven to 400°F. Spread the bell peppers, then the zucchini and eggplant in a large, shallow roasting pan or baking sheet, keeping them all separate. Drizzle the eggplant with 1 tablespoon of the oil and the bell peppers and zucchini with another 1 tablespoon between them. Toss well so that they are all coated in the oil, still keeping them separate and in a single layer, then season with black pepper and a little salt. Roast for 30–35 minutes or until softened and tinged brown.

2 Meanwhile, make a tomato sauce. Wrap the thyme and rosemary in the bay leaf to make a bouquet garni and tie up with kitchen string. Heat the 2 teaspoons oil in a large saucepan or sauté pan. Add the onion and garlic and sauté on medium-low heat for about 10 minutes, until softened but not browned, stirring occasionally. Halve the tomatoes, cut out their cores, then coarsely chop. Stir the tomatoes and the bouquet garni in with the onion and cook, still on low heat, for 20–25 minutes or until of a sauce consistency.

3 Add the roasted vegetables to the tomato sauce, scraping the juices in, too. Stir in the crushed coriander, then cover and warm through briefly to bring everything together, but still keeping the shape of the vegetables. Remove the bouquet garni, season with more black pepper, if needed, and sprinkle with the chopped cilantro and parsley to serve.

TIP

• Although usually served as a warm or hot vegetable accompaniment, ratatouille is also good served at room temperature as a light lunch or dinner. Though it will up the fat slightly, a little crumbled feta cheese sprinkled over the top makes it quite substantial.

Flavor with coriander seeds and you won't need much salt

Creamed garlicky spinach

Toss spinach in a creamy sauce and you have a special vegetable side dish, but with butter and cream used to enrich the sauce, fat levels can be high. I've come up with a flavorsome, creamy sauce that needs neither of those ingredients, and calories and fats are more than halved.

	Classic	Lighter
Kcals	192	83
Fat	12.9 g	3.1 g
Sat fat	7.7 g	1.6 g
Sodium	320 mg	240 mg

Per serving 83 kcals

Protein 5.5 g, carbs 8.3 g, fat 3.1 g, sat fat 1.6 g, fiber 3.1 g, sugar 4.8 g, sodium 240 mg

Serves 4

Prep: 15 minutes
Cook: 15 minutes

1 tablespoon cornstarch

1 cup low-fat milk

2 garlic cloves, finely chopped

1 large or 2 small shallots, minced

14 oz (about 13⅓ cups) spinach leaves

good pinch of grated nutmeg, plus extra to garnish

2 tablespoons reduced-fat crème fraîche or Greek yogurt

salt and freshly ground black pepper

1 Mix the cornstarch with 1 tablespoon of the milk in a small bowl and set aside. Pour the rest of the milk into a medium saucepan. Drop in the chopped garlic and shallot, bring just to a boil, then lower the heat and simmer gently for 6–8 minutes to soften them. Set aside to steep.

2 Meanwhile, put the spinach in a large, heatproof bowl and pour almost boiling water over the leaves. Let stand for 30–45 seconds to wilt, turning it in the water as it sits. Drain off the water and put the spinach into a colander. Let stand for a minute or two to finish off wilting, turning it over occasionally, then, when cool enough to handle (if it's not, refresh it quickly under cold running water and drain), squeeze out any excess water really well with the back of a wooden spoon or your hands. Chop the spinach.

3 Restir the cornstarch mix, then stir it into the steeped milk. Put the saucepan on the heat and bring to a boil, stirring until thickened and smooth. Remove from the heat, then season with black pepper, a small pinch of salt, and the nutmeg. Stir in the crème fraîche.

4 Stir the spinach into the sauce and warm through briefly on low heat. If heated for too long, the spinach will lose its vibrant color. Serve sprinkled with an extra pinch of nutmeg to garnish.

Reduce fat by making a butterless sauce with cornstarch and milk, steeped with shallot and garlic to boost the taste

Potato Dauphinoise

Potato Dauphinoise, or scalloped potatoes, relies on butter, milk, and cream for its richness. What makes this dish hard to adapt is that the recipe also relies on the potatoes cooking in these ingredients to create a creamy sauce, but I've made this lighter version just as special.

	Classic	Lighter
Kcals	424	232
Fat	32.3 g	12 g
Sat fat	18.4 g	7 g
Sodium	328 mg	100 mg

Per serving 232 kcals

Protein 6 g, carbs 27 g, fat 12 g, sat fat 7 g, fiber 2 g, sugar 3 g, sodium 100 mg

Serves 6

Prep: 30 minutes, plus infusing
Cook: about 1½ hours

1 teaspoon olive oil

⅔ cup low-fat milk

1 plump garlic clove, peeled and halved

4 sprigs of thyme, plus extra small sprigs for sprinkling

1 bay leaf

1 shallot, coarsely chopped

good pinch of freshly grated nutmeg

5 red-skinned or white round potatoes

⅔ cup crème fraîche or Greek yogurt

⅓ cup vegetable stock

1 teaspoon thyme leaves

¼ cup shredded Gruyère cheese or a vegetarian alternative

salt and freshly ground black pepper

1 Preheat the oven to 325°F. Brush the oil over the bottom and sides of a 10 x 7 x 2 inch ovenproof dish. Put the milk, garlic, the 4 sprigs of thyme, bay leaf, and shallot into a saucepan. Bring just to a boil, then remove from the heat and add the nutmeg and a little black pepper. Set aside to steep while you prepare the potatoes.

2 Peel, then slice the potatoes thinly. Pat them dry. Layer half of the slices in the dish, overlapping slightly, then season with black pepper and a little salt.

3 Strain the steeped milk into a small bowl. Put the crème fraîche into a bowl, then gradually pour in the milk, whisking until smooth. Add the stock and thyme leaves. Return this liquid to the small bowl, then pour half of it over the potatoes in the dish.

4 Layer the rest of the potatoes in the dish, then add the remaining liquid, the cheese, and a grind of black pepper. Sit the dish on a baking sheet and bake for 1¼–1½ hours, until golden and tender—test by inserting a sharp knife through the potatoes. Let it stand for 5 minutes before serving, sprinkled with small sprigs of thyme.

Lower fat by eliminating cream and butter. use crème fraîche combined with stock and low-fat milk instead

Pesto

There are many versions of this fragrantly flavored Italian sauce, but most require a lot of oil, high-fat pine nuts and Parmesan. However, it wouldn't be a classic pesto without them, so by introducing fewer high-fat ingredients to complement and bulk out the traditional ones, saturated fat is greatly reduced but it still tastes like the real thing.

	Classic	Lighter
Kcals	91	56
Fat	9.1 g	5.6 g
Sat fat	1.7 g	0.8 g
Sodium	40 mg	40 mg

Per tablespoon 56 kcals

Protein 1.2 g, carbs 0.3 g, fat 5.6 g, sat fat 0.8 g, fiber 0.3 g, sugar 0.2 g, sodium 40 mg

Makes 1¼ cups

Prep: 10 minutes
Cook: 5 minutes

3 tablespoons pine nuts

3 oz baby broccoli spears

1 cup basil

¼ cup finely diced Parmesan cheese

2 garlic cloves, coarsely chopped

3 tablespoons olive oil

2 tablespoons canola oil, plus 1 teaspoon

salt and freshly ground black pepper

1 Toast the pine nuts in a small, heavy saucepan over medium heat until golden, moving them around in the pan often so that they brown evenly. Set aside.

2 Chop the broccoli spears finely and put them in a small saucepan of boiling water to blanch. Bring back to a boil, then cook for 2 minutes so that the broccoli still has some bite and keeps its color. Immediately, drain the broccoli in a strainer and put under cold running water to stop it from cooking and keep its freshness. Drain well.

3 Strip the leaves from the basil stems and put them in the food processor with the pine nuts, Parmesan, and garlic. Pulse briefly to combine and coarsely chop. Add the broccoli, and with the machine running, pour in the olive oil and the 2 tablespoons of canola oil. Don't overprocess the mixture, because you want to keep some texture. Season with a little black pepper and a pinch of salt.

4 Transfer to a bowl and pour over the extra 1 teaspoon of canola oil to protect the surface. It will keep in the refrigerator for 3–4 days. It also freezes well.

Toast the pine nuts to heighten their flavor, then use fewer to reduce fat farther and let baby broccoli spears provide any loss of bulk.

Red onion marmalade

As with any preserves, sugar is bound to be high, and because the onions are traditionally fried to caramelize them, fat can be high, too. To bring the sugar levels down by nearly half, I've found other ways to sweeten this marmalade, and to reduce the fat, I've completely changed the way it is cooked, yet the taste is still great and the texture irresistibly sticky.

	Classic	Lighter
Kcals	27	14
Fat	1.2 g	0.4 g
Sat fat	0.3 g	0 g
Sugar	3.2 g	1.8 g
Sodium	40 mg	0 g

Per tablespoon 14 kcals

Protein 0.3 g, carbs 2.2 g, fat 0.4 g, sat fat 0g, fiber 0.4 g, sugar 1.8 g, sodium 0 g

Makes about 2⅓ cups

Prep: 25 minutes
Cook: about 1 hour

4 red onions, peeled

3 garlic cloves, chopped

1½ teaspoons mustard seeds

2 sprigs of thyme

¼ teaspoon salt

1½ tablespoons canola oil

2 tablespoons packed light brown sugar

2 teaspoons black molasses

¼ cup dry white wine

2 tablespoons red wine vinegar

1 tablespoon balsamic vinegar

freshly ground black pepper

1 Preheat the oven to 375°F. Halve the onions lengthwise, then slice thinly with the cut side facing down. Put the onions, garlic, mustard seeds, and thyme sprigs in a large roasting pan. Sprinkle with the salt and a good grinding of black pepper. Pour in the oil and toss together with your hands to coat well. Spread the onions out in a single layer and roast for about 40 minutes, stirring twice, until well reduced and softened. Increase the oven temperature to 400°F and roast for another 15–20 minutes, until the onions are starting to stick and caramelize on the bottom of the pan.

2 Remove from the oven, discard the thyme sprigs, and stir in the sugar, molasses, wine, and both vinegars. Transfer the onion mixture and any juices to a medium saucepan. Rinse the roasting pan out with ⅓ cup of water and stir these juices into the onions in the saucepan. Bring the mixture up to a gentle simmer and let it cook for about 5 minutes or until the juices get a little sticky.

3 Spoon the onion marmalade into small, clean, sterilized lidded glass jars. It will keep for at least a month in the refrigerator.

choose red onions for their natural sweet flavor so that added sugar can be reduced and calories lowered

Scotch eggs

This lighter version of "Scotch" eggs enwrapped in ground pork and bread crumbs involves substituting some of the meat with lentils and pan-frying before baking. These are best eaten the day they are made.

	Classic	Lighter
Kcals	529	223
Fat	42.6 g	11.7 g
Sat fat	9.3 g	2.6 g
Sodium	2 g	200 mg

Per Scotch egg 223 kcals

Protein 21 g, carbs 8.3 g, fat 11.7 g, sat fat 2.6 g, fiber 1.4 g, sugar 0.3 g, sodium 200 mg

Makes 4

Prep: 40 minutes, plus cooling
    and chilling
Cook: 25 minutes

5 teaspoons canola oil

1 shallot, finely chopped

5 large eggs

⅓ cup canned or cooked green lentils

8 oz less than 5% fat ground pork

2 teaspoons finely chopped sage

3 teaspoons finely snipped chives

½ teaspoon dry English mustard

good pinch of grated nutmeg

1 tablespoon all-purpose flour

¼ cup Japanese panko bread crumbs

salt and freshly ground black pepper

1 Heat 1 teaspoon of the oil in a small, nonstick skillet. Add the shallot and sauté for a few minutes until softened. Transfer to a plate and set aside to cool. (No need to wash the pan, because you can use it later.)

2 Meanwhile, put 4 of the eggs in a medium saucepan, covering well with cold water. Bring to a boil—as the water starts to boil, set the timer and boil for 5 minutes. When cooked, pour off a boiling water and cool the eggs under cold running water to stop them from cooking farther.

3 Mash the lentils well in a medium bowl with the back of a fork, then stir in the ground pork, sage, 2 teaspoons of the chives, the dry mustard, nutmeg, cooled shallots, a pinch of salt, and a generous grating of black pepper. Peel the shells from the eggs and pat dry with paper towels.

4 Divide the meat mixture evenly into 4. Put the flour onto a plate and roll each egg in it to coat, tapping off any excess. Pat down one-quarter of the meat mixture on the work surface to a 4½–5 inch circle, using the rest of the flour to keep it from sticking. Cup the disk in your hand and place one of the eggs in the center. Using both hands, pat, press, and ease the meat mixture around the egg until it is completely and evenly covered. Seal really well so that there is no seam, then pat and roll it into a good shape on the floured surface. Repeat with the rest of the meat mixture and cooked eggs.

5 Mix the panko crumbs on a large plate with the remaining chives. Beat the remaining egg on a plate, brush some all over each coated egg (you won't use it all), then roll the eggs in the panko crumbs, patting them on to stick. Lay the eggs on a baking sheet lined with parchment paper and chill for 20–25 minutes (but not overnight). Preheat the oven to 375°F.

6 Heat 2 teaspoons of the remaining oil in the saucepan you used for the shallot. When hot (it is hot enough when a few panko crumbs dropped in sizzle immediately and start to brown), put in 2 of the Scotch eggs and roll in the oil to coat them well. Set the timer for 2 minutes, and cook the eggs, turning often, to brown all over. You are just browning, not fully cooking the eggs at this stage, so don't overcook or the coating may start to split. Transfer to the lined baking sheet and repeat with the remaining eggs and oil, lowering the heat slightly if the pan gets too hot.

7 Bake the Scotch eggs for 12 minutes. Remove, lay them on paper towels to drain, and let cool slightly.

use extra-lean ground pork and large eggs instead of extra-large to reduce fat, and swap some of the meat for lentils

•

Pan-fry and bake instaed of deep-fry the eggs to reduce fat even more

Creamy mashed potatoes

Even without a lot of butter and whole milk, this recipe still makes a soft, creamy mashed potatoes—the perfect accompaniment to roasted or broiled chicken, and many other family favorites.

	Classic	Lighter
Kcals	408	225
Fat	24.7 g	4.1 g
Sat fat	15.2 g	2.4 g
Sodium	120 mg	40 mg

Per serving 225 kcals

Protein 6.3 g, carbs 40.5 g, fat 4.1 g, sat fat 2.4 g, fiber 3.3 g, sugar 2.3 g, sodium 40 mg

Serves 6

Prep: 10 minutes
Cook: 15 minutes

13 russet or Yukon gold potatoes, cut into even chunks

½ cup low-fat milk

1 tablespoon butter

¼ cup reduced-fat crème fraîche or Greek yogurt

salt and freshly ground black pepper

1 Bring a large saucepan of water to a boil. Add the potatoes and boil for about 15 minutes or until tender. Transfer to a colander and drain well, then return to the pan and set over low heat for 2 minutes to dry completely.

2 Heat the milk and butter in a small saucepan, then pour the liquid over the potatoes. Remove the pan from the heat, then mash the potatoes using an electric hand mixer or potato masher. Add the crème fraîche and beat with a wooden spoon until smooth and creamy. Season with black pepper and a pinch of salt.

Lower the fat and calories by replacing butter with lower-fat milk and reduced-fat crème fraîche

TIPS FOR MAKING IT LIGHTER

Tips for making it lighter

In choosing and using the recipes in this book, you will have seen that each and every one of them employs at least one way or another of substantially reducing the fat, salt, or sugar content of a dish. The methods are quite simple and uncomplicated in many cases, and yet the reduction in calories between one of my lighter dishes and its classic equivalent is often dramatic. As you gain in confidence, you'll be able use the same tricks to adapt classic dishes of your own. Here are some of the best.

TEN WAYS WITH ... Meat and fish

- Choose lean cuts of meat for your dishes.

- Trim off excess fat and remove skin from fish and chicken.

- For recipes that call for lardons or chopped bacon, use thick slices of ham instead, trimmed of all fat.

- By using poached salmon instead of smoked salmon for a given recipe, you can greatly reduce the sodium intake.

- To enhance the flavor of chicken, pork, lamb, or fish, marinate in yogurt and spices or oil and herbs before cooking.

- Rub meat with a mix of dried spices prior to cooking. That way, you'll eliminate any need for salt.

- Mix extra vegetables such as grated raw carrot into ground meat, or use green lentils to add bulk and reduce the amount of meat you need.

- Always use a nonstick pan for cooking meat and fish. That way you'll need less oil.

- Better still, if you can broil or grill meat or fish instead of pan-frying it, you'll need even less oil.

- Instead of serving burgers, fish, or chicken with store-bought sauces, make your own fresh fruit or vegetable salsas.

... Fruit, vegetables, and nuts

- Don't bother salting eggplants. It is no longer necessary now that newer varieties are less bitter.

- Boost your fiber intake by leaving the peel on apples and potatoes whenever it is possible.

- Always use soft fruits when in season. They will have the best flavor and be at their sweetest, so you can use less sugar.

- For a change of pace, replace regular potato with sweet potato or celeriac, or use half and half.

- Cut down on carbohydrates by serving smaller pasta and rice portions, but bumping them up with peas, carrots, bell peppers, or zucchini.

- Replace salt entirely using dried porcini, fresh herbs, mustard, garlic, Tabasco sauce, crushed dried chiles, lemon, or lime. Almost any savory recipe can use at least one of these great taste boosters.

- Cover the top of cheesy or pasta casseroles with halved cherry tomatoes.

- Steam vegetables whenever possible to minimize nutrient loss.

- Roast instead of fry vegetables to keep fat to a minimum.

- Dry-roast raw nuts and whole spices—it intensifies their flavor.

FIVE WAYS WITH ... Dairy and eggs

- By choosing strong-tasting cheeses such as Parmesan, you'll find you need less of them.

- Steep milk for savory sauces with herbs, garlic, and shallots, and cut out the salt altogether.

- Replace high-fat creams with reduced-fat crème fraîche combined with plain yogurt.

- Use large eggs, not extra-large, when appropriate.

- Instead of using cream as a base for a pasta sauce, save some of the cooking water.

... Baked goods and desserts

- Replace some of the butter with plain yogurt and canola oil when making pastry or cakes.

- Line baking sheets with parchment paper instead of greasing them with oil or butter.

- When making mousses, replace an egg yolk with whisked egg white for a lower-fat way of increasing volume.

- Use unrefined sugars. For a fudgier taste, mix light or dark brown sugar with golden granulated sugar.

- Choose good-quality bittersweet chocolate (70% cocoa solids) for its depth of flavor. A little unsweetened cocoa powder can replace some of the chocolate, but avoid adding too much, because it will give a powdery taste.

Winning substitutes

Canola oil for other oils
Why? It is lower in saturated fat (containing less than half that of olive oil).

Green or brown lentils for ground meat
Why? It reduces saturated fat dramatically when used half and half. It also increases fiber.

Phyllo pastry for traditional pastry toppings
Why? It is lower in calories, fat, and carbohydrates.

Whole-wheat flour for white
Why? It increases fiber and is richer in some nutrients, such as the B vitamins. A good ratio is half and half with white (using all whole wheat can make a mixture heavy).

Watercress and arugula for lettuce
Why? Darker leaves tend to be richer in nutrients such as betacarotene.

Calorie countdown

How often do you look at the back of a package when shopping to see how many calories a given product has? Calorie counting has become a way of life for many of us and shows that we care about the number of calories we consume, and that, wherever possible, we want to keep within the daily recommended guidelines given on page 10.

The following countdown presents all of the recipes in this book that are below 600 calories, from the highest to the lowest. Whether you are looking for a light lunch, an impressive dessert, or a dinner to share with the family, the list will help you to make a calorie-conscious choice in no time.

Recipes under 700 calories

609 Kcals: Paella, page 119
618 Kcals: The Full English Breakfast, page 190
649 Kcals: Fish and Chips, page 46

Recipes under 600 calories

527 Kcals: Spaghetti Carbonara, page 94
517 Kcals: Risotto with Squash and Sage, page 40
515 Kcals: Chicken Tikka Masala, page 80
511 Kcals: Beef Turnovers, page 198
503 Kcals: Macaroni and Cheese, page 64

Recipes under 500 calories

498 Kcals: Pizza Margherita, page 72
487 Kcals: Thai Green Chicken Curry, page 86
485 Kcals: Chicken Biryani, page 116
475 Kcals: Risotto Primavera, page 104
451 Kcals: Salad Niçoise, page 28
447 Kcals: Lasagne, page 54
430 Kcals: Chicken Caesar Salad, page 24
429 Kcals: Shepherd's Pie, page 70
420 Kcals: Coq au Vin, page 98
413 Kcals: Fish Casserole, page 112
405 Kcals: French Onion Soup, page 16

405 Kcals: Nasi Goreng, page 96
405 Kcals: Burgers with Roasted Pepper Salsa, page 74
402 Kcals: Chicken Korma, page 52
402 Kcals: Coronation Chicken, page 32

Recipes under 400 calories

398 Kcals: Fish Chowder, page 36
373 Kcals: Steak and Kidney Pie, page 58
359 Kcals: Syrupy Sponge Cake, page 133
353 Kcals: Apple and Blackberry Crisp, page 148
350 Kcals: Beef Wellington, page 108
339 Kcals: Lamb Tagine, page 101
336 Kcals: Coffee and Walnut Cake, page 164
335 Kcals: Fish Chowder, page 36
331 Kcals: Salmon en Croûte, page 90
325 Kcals: Moussaka, page 42
320 Kcals: Chicken Pie, page 66
319 Kcals: Crispy Chicken, page 60
318 Kcals: Fruity Sponge Cake and Custard, page 130
315 Kcals: New York Cheesecake, page 122
312 Kcals: Bread and Butter Pudding, page 150
309 Kcals: Onion Tart, page 78

Recipes under 300 calories

298 Kcals: Shrimp Laksa, page 22
295 Kcals: Spanish Omelet, page 193
280 Kcals: Almond Tart, page 186
272 Kcals: Quiche Lorraine, page 50
271 Kcals: Chocolate Log, page 172
270 Kcals: Coffee Panna Cotta, page 125
269 Kcals: Salmon Teriyaki, page 102
263 Kcals: Raspberry Sponge Cake, page 182
262 Kcals: Chicken Cacciatore, page 83
260 Kcals: Apple Tart, page 143
257 Kcals: Crème Brûlée, page 154
255 Kcals: Mediterranean Fish Stew, page 103
254 Kcals: Greek Salad, page 35
247 Kcals: Shoofly Pie, page 167
243 Kcals: Chocolate Tart, page 126
243 Kcals: Lemon Drizzle Cake, page 168
239 Kcals: Fish Cakes, page 49
236 Kcals: Crunchy Granola, page 192
234 Kcals: Chocolate Cupcakes, page 177
232 Kcals: Potato Dauphinoise, page 206
230 Kcals: Pork Stir-Fry, page 57
225 Kcals: Creamy Mashed Potatoes, page 213
223 Kcals: Scotch Eggs, page 210
220 Kcals: Tiramisu, page 134
217 Kcals: Chicken Balti, page 89
217 Kcals: Carrot Cake, page 160
215 Kcals: Potato Salad, page 30
213 Kcals: Creamy Butternut Squash Soup, page 27
213 Kcals: Eggplant Parmigiana, page 111
206 Kcals: Blueberry Muffins, page 178

Recipes under 200 calories

196 Kcals: Strawberry Ice Cream Milk Shake, page 152
194 Kcals: Banana Bread, page 171
191 Kcals: Chocolate Brownies, page 162
186 Kcals: Lemon Tart, page 138
186 Kcals: Shrimp Cocktail, page 14
180 Kcals: Raspberry and Passion Fruit Meringe, page 153
175 Kcals: Twice-Baked Cheese Soufflés, page 18
169 Kcals: StrawberryWhip, page 129
167 Kcals: Chocolate Mousse, page 146
162 Kcals: Semifreddo with Summer Fruits, page 149
161 Kcals: Ratatouille, page 204
160 Kcals: Garlic Bread, page 201
157 Kcals: Salmon Pâté, page 21
157 Kcals: Oatmeal Bars, page 184
148 Kcals: Vanilla Ice Cream, page 144
145 Kcals: Hummus, page 195
141 Kcals: Leek and Potato Soup, page 29
141 Kcals: Roasted Vegetables, page 194
130 Kcals: Sticky Gingerbread, page 170
116 Kcals: Oat and Raisin Cookies, page 185
106 Kcals: Peanut Butter Cookies, page 176
99 Kcals: Sausage Rolls, page 196
97 Kcals: Chocolate Chip Cookies, page 180
94 Kcals: Crunchy Coleslaw, page 63
83 Kcals: Creamed Garlicky Spinach, page 205
56 Kcals: Braised Leeks and Peas, page 202
56 Kcals: Pesto, page 208
14 Kcals: Red Onion Marmalade, page 209

Index

I dedicate this book to Elizabeth, Emily, and Megan.
May it give them as much inspiration as they give to me.

Acknowledgments

A big thank you to all my friends, "the tasters," who have given their unbiased opinions when sampling these recipes with me. I'm grateful for all of your comments. I am indebted to registered nutritional therapist Kerry Torrens, who provided support and invaluable nutritional advice. She also analyzed the new recipes for the book and calculated all the "health alerts." Thank you, Kerry – I couldn't have done it without you. Thanks, too, to nutritionists Wendy Doyle and Fiona Hunter, whose expertise I greatly valued while working on the original recipes for *BBC Good Food* magazine. I'd also like to thank the editorial team at *Good Food*, especially the magazine's editor, Gillian Carter, who supported my idea for this book and continues to encourage a healthier way of eating in the magazine. And lastly, many thanks to Octopus Publishing Group for agreeing to publish this book and to the editorial and design team for making it look as good as it does.

Commissioning editor Eleanor Maxfield
Deputy art director Yasia Williams-Leedham
Design Jaz Bahra
Editors Alex Stetter and Katy Denny
Production controller Sarah Kramer

Photo credits

David Munns, apart from the following:
Lara Holmes 37, 155
Gareth Morgans 71
Stuart Ovenden 183
Lis Parsons 67–9, 81, 177, 207
Philip Webb 139 (finished tart), 211
Simon Wheeler 25, 47, 51, 123, 191

Food styling

Angela Nilsen, apart from the following:
Lizzie Harris 37, 211
Jane Hornby 139 (finished tart), 183
Jennifer Joyce 155
Lucy O'Reilly 61